What Do You Seek?

Welcoming the Adult Inquirer

What Do You Seek?

Welcoming the Adult Inquirer

Augsburg Fortress

Minneapolis

Cover art: Tanja Butler
General editor: Dennis Bushkofsky
Editors: Suzanne Burke, Rebecca Lowe

Also available:
Welcome to Christ: A Lutheran Introduction to the Catechumenate (3-140) ISBN 0-8066-3393-X
Welcome to Christ: A Lutheran Catechetical Guide (3-141) ISBN 0-8066-3394-8
Welcome to Christ: Lutheran Rites for the Catechumenate (3-142) ISBN 0-8066-3395-6

The paper used in this publication meets the minimum requirements of American National Standards for Information Sciences—Permanence of Paper for Printed Library materials, ANSI Z329.48-1984.

Manufactured in the USA   ISBN 0-8066-4031-6   AFP 3-4031
07 06 05 04 03 02 01   2 3 4 5 6 7 8 9 10

Contents

Contributors

Jeffrey Anderson (Chapter 4) is a member of St. Paul Lutheran Church in Durham, North Carolina.

Dennis Bushkofsky (Chapter 1; general editor) is a Lutheran pastor who lives in Bloomington, Minnesota.

Robert Hofstad (Chapter 7) is Assistant to the Bishop of the Southwestern Washington Synod of the Evangelical Lutheran Church in America.

Frank Honeycutt (Chapter 2) is pastor of St. John Lutheran Church in Abingdon, Virginia.

Clement Mehlman (Chapter 3) is a Lutheran campus chaplain in Nova Scotia and serves on the Task Force on the Adult Catechumenate of the Evangelical Lutheran Church in Canada.

Michael Mills (Chapter 6) is pastor of Advent Lutheran Church in North York, Ontario.

Beverly Piro (Chapter 5) is a Lutheran pastor who lives in Seattle, Washington.

Roger Prehn (review team) is pastor of St. Paul Lutheran Church in Orlando, Florida.

Richard L. Stetson (review team) is Assistant to the Bishop of the Evangelical Lutheran Church in Canada.

Karen Ward (liturgical resources in appendixes; review team) is Associate Director for Worship in the Division for Congregational Ministries of the Evangelical Lutheran Church in America.

Introduction

New members. Every congregation wants them. We may even pray to have them, especially if we believe that having more of them will help us brighten our church's financial picture. Much of the time we also appreciate the vitality and the openness to new ideas that new members bring with them. Ministering effectively to new members, however, requires a great amount of energy and human resources. When we get right down to it, each person comes from a different background and has unique needs in relating to a congregation for the first time.

While we may be able to plan some events and learning opportunities that will be suitable for most new members, many people who care for new members discover quickly that there is no one-size-fits-all new member program. Every congregation must devise a plan for receiving new members that will work for its own setting and potential. Meanwhile, the needs of one who may be transferring his or her membership from another congregation will likely be vastly different from the needs of a person who has never had an active life in the church before—whether baptized or not.

Though receiving new members is one of the more joyful responsibilities of congregational life, it is also one of the most difficult tasks to do well. New members rarely come all at once. And even if they did arrive together, they would still present us with a myriad of needs that would make us feel thoroughly unprepared for the task.

This book addresses those challenges. The following chapters examine a process for receiving new members that has proven to accommodate a variety of needs. This book acknowledges that Joe at age seventy—who has been an active church member for all his adult life, has taught Bible classes in a former congregation, and is now transferring his membership to a congregation in a new retirement community—has quite different needs from Maria, the thirty-year-old mother who is seeking out the church for the very first time in her life because it offers a place to impart some helpful values to her young children.

Maria and Joe may both have similar needs when it comes to relating to a new group of people and learning the idiosyncrasies of their new congregation. But they have different needs in their respective faith journeys. Maria admits that her faith journey is just beginning. Though baptized at a young age, her family lived in six different states before she left home to go to college, and never really established any long-lasting church relationship. Maria's knowledge of the scriptures is spotty. She would not be able to tell the difference between

Noah and Jonah. She knows that there is more than one gospel in the Bible, but she would not be able to identify all of them correctly if the names of the books were scrambled. Joe could be a mentor to Maria as she seeks out an active life in the church. Joe knows enough about the Bible and Christian doctrine to be able to pass seminary tests. His recent retirement has now given him a great deal of extra time, and he is hoping to find one or more areas of volunteer service in his new congregation and in the community at large.

What might confront Maria and Joe in a typical congregation's new members program? You, the reader, would best know what might be offered for each of them if they were in your congregation. In this imaginary situation, Maria and Joe have been invited to come to an informal dinner hosted by several members on a given Sunday evening. Joe is familiar with the process—he often helped serve meals like this one in his previous congregation. He is hoping to be able to meet up with other recent retirees at the dinner. Maria, meanwhile, is interested in meeting other young parents. She appreciates the opportunity to get to know several people in the congregation before she becomes a member, but she has many questions that are going through her mind. What is the Bible all about? How do people learn how to pray? How can she answer her children's questions about God?

Will Joe and Maria find what they each are seeking? Will it happen in a single evening? Do they even know for sure what it is that they are seeking? Will someone in their new congregation care to ask them, "What do you seek?"

What do you seek? It is a question that will come back in this volume. It is a question that this book will encourage you to ask in many different ways in your congregation's new member process. Those who have contributed to this volume have served congregations that use extensive new member processes. These processes are tailored and re-tailored to meet the needs of new members who come from a variety of backgrounds, seeking a wide range of what the church has to offer. No two groups of new members are ever alike, though some basic patterns are helpful in many situations. And the patterns can be altered so that congregations have a response for newcomers when they answer one of the first questions: "What do you seek?"

Chapter 1

Who Are Inquirers?

Whatever name we may use to describe them—inquirers, seekers, new members—they are people who come to our congregations with diverse experiences and a wide range of previous exposure (or lack thereof) to the church, the scriptures, and Christian beliefs in general. Many of us may be looking for the one thing that will help us minister to inquirers of all types equally well. Is it realistic that we will ever find the one resource for all circumstances? This book proposes an answer to that question. But first let us examine the situations of many different types of persons who may be seeking membership in the church.

Receiving Members by Transfer

When people have recently been active members of another congregation—either within the same denomination or a similar Christian tradition—we may receive them by "letter of transfer" from another congregation. When such persons come into a new congregation, their primary needs may be to get to know other members and learn some of the basic ways that the new congregation is organized and does its work.

While newcomers may not be interested in learning about a congregation's committee structure or system of governance right away, they probably will want to know about opportunities for service and spiritual nurture that the congregation supports. They need an appropriate orientation session to the new congregation and some kind of personal attention that can help them to be integrated into the congregation's life. A catalog or list of ministry opportunities, a monthly newsletter, a membership directory, a sponsor who will help them in getting acquainted, and some special attention from the church staff during their first few months of interest in the congregation will prove to be helpful.

If newcomers are familiar with basic worship patterns of their new congregation, and if they understand the new congregation's beliefs (especially if it is within the same or similar denominational family from which they have come), persons who are to be received by transfer from another congregation may need little else beyond what has been mentioned in the previous paragraph. They should be introduced to the congregation soon after they have decided to join, and they should be given the charge to support the church as is expected of all members. They should also be encouraged to participate in the congregation's small group ministry.

This is the category that Joe is in (someone we met in the introduction). Joe has already spent many years active in the life of another congregation. While he is interested in getting acclimated to Grace Church (his new congregation), he does not need a primer on the scriptures or on Christian faith. He does seek to be connected to a discipleship group in his new congregation.

Candidates for Baptism

At the other end of the new member spectrum from Joe is Fran. She is a middle-aged woman who has not been baptized and has never been involved in a church before. Fran was recently married to a person who is already a member of Grace Church. She was intrigued by the marriage service and the whole process of getting married in the church. She recognizes that she needs to start from the beginning, having never before attended a Sunday school class, picked up a Bible, or sung hymns.

Fran has lots of questions about God. In many ways she feels that she does not even know enough to ask an intelligent question. Her husband is constantly amazed by what she does not know about Christian teachings, and often gets frustrated by questions that he has not heard in years. How is Fran to be helped by her new congregation?

Candidates for Affirmation

In between Joe and Fran on the new member spectrum is a wide range of people with a huge assortment of needs and expectations about their new congregation. One new member is Maria (who we also met in the introduction). Though Maria has been baptized, her spiritual development needs are not all that different from those of Fran. Maria is seeking a church home especially for her young children. She called Grace Church asking if the children could be baptized, and the pastor set up a time to meet with Maria and her two preschool-aged children. The pastor arranged for a new member sponsor to also join them at the meeting.

As Maria's children are prepared for baptism, she needs to be introduced to the scriptures, become better aware of the church's worship patterns, and learn a pattern of prayer that will serve her own needs and those of her growing children. Maria hopes to become involved in a variety of church activities some day, but she needs an environment where she can start at the beginning ("Church for Dummies" is what she had asked for in the meeting with the pastor and her prospective sponsor).

Juan and Diane are a couple who have moved into the area recently and worshiped at Grace Church one Sunday. On the friendship pad that was passed down the pew, they checked the "interested in membership" column. When a member of Grace Church's hospitality team called them up the next day, she found out that Juan and Diane had each attended churches of different denominations when they were growing up. They are planning to get married in about a year and have been looking for a church where they could get married. Though they have never before attended a church of the denomination that Grace Church is a part of, Juan and Diane like what they have seen and are eager to get involved in what seems to be a very friendly congregation.

Ken is yet another person who has signed the friendship pad in recent weeks. He just recently returned to the country after spending six years overseas working for a multinational corporation as it began an operation in Asia. Ken has only rarely attended church throughout the past decade. Though confirmed at sixteen, he remembers very little of what he learned in church at that time. He is hoping that Grace Church will allow him to explore some of the spiritual yearnings he has been having lately. He also expects that the church will be a good place to meet people outside of work, which takes up a good deal of his time these days.

Identifying Needs

What do Joe, Fran, Maria, Juan, Diane, and Ken seek? They all seek to be involved in a local congregation in some way, and they have all sought out Grace Church in particular. Their wide range of experiences will not make it easy to address all of their needs in one tidy program or single new member curriculum. We could discern at least three distinctly different sets of needs in this group of people who have all been identified as prospective new members within a month or two of each other. Joe is eager to participate right away, and has the ability to volunteer as a leader in the congregation's adult education program. Fran and Maria need to start at the beginning with a program that assumes nothing about their faith background. Meanwhile, Juan, Diane, and Ken each have a history of church involvement that can provide a basis for reflection as each one connects or reconnects with the Christian faith and its community.

After a new member sponsor has been assigned to each of the persons we have mentioned, they are invited to become a part of a group that will meet each of their needs. Joe is invited into the Bible study leaders group, where he will be joining two other newly recruited small group leaders. He looks forward to serving as a Bible study leader himself in his new congregation. The coordinator of the study groups offers to serve as Joe's sponsor and to introduce Joe to other members of the congregation. Joe will be received by letter of transfer from his previous congregation in about a month.

After being assigned new member sponsors, Fran and Maria are invited to join a new group of inquirers that will be starting up in a few weeks. The inquirers will have many opportunities to ask some basic questions and to explore Christian teachings at the beginner level. They will participate in an order of "Welcome of Inquirers" on a Sunday in October, even though their inquirers group is just beginning. The group will continue to meet for as long as each of them need it. Fran, who has not been baptized, will be a "catechumen," while Maria will be an "affirmer," since she was baptized as a child.

Meanwhile, Juan, Diane, and Ken have been invited into a small group of affirmers, who each have a sponsor. The first meeting of the affirmers group begins with a recollection of baptism and with each person charting a story of their own life of faith. The time frame for this group is somewhat open-ended, though they have been asked to commit to at least a twelve-week period of time, in which they will attend worship each week. They will meet after the service each week for a seventy-five-minute session that reflects on the scriptures for the week, then turns to a brief conversation about a specific Christian teaching, and concludes with prayer.

The leaders of the new member process at Grace Church have identified what each of these six new people need (Maria's two children actually bring the total to eight—they have begun Sunday school classes). The new member process is designed to be flexible enough to address a variety of needs, while still grouping people together. Grace Church depends upon several guides (leaders of small groups) and sponsors to assist in the work of introducing newcomers to the church and to the Christian faith. A new member leadership team supports the work of all those involved in the process. The pastor meets each of the newcomers within a week or two of their expressed interest in the church, and greets each of them warmly following worship services and at fellowship events of the congregation. Much of the work done on behalf of each newcomer is provided by the one-on-one sponsor relationship and the leader for each of the small groups.

Guide for Affirmers

This book is intentionally designed as a guide for working with *affirmers*. In other words, the guide is intended to help congregations prepare inquirers or newcomers for Affirmation of Baptism. Affirmers are baptized people with a diverse range of experiences who seek life in a congregation or who are interested in renewing their faith.

One group of affirmers may be people who wish to reconnect with the church after a prolonged absence (perhaps they grew up in the church, but they moved, lost interest, or were alienated from it for a variety of reasons). Affirmers may also be people who are already members of congregations, but now wish to deepen their faith in a deliberate process. A life change such as divorce, death of a loved one, retirement, engagement, or a variety of other circumstances may be an appropriate occasion for an affirmation of baptism (see appendix E, Excerpts from *The Use of the Means of Grace*, p. 74).

Congregations may also use the affirmer model presented here for confirmation of youth. In fact, the ministry with affirmers as outlined in this volume is compatible with many trends in adolescent confirmation: small group learning, mentoring, and blending hands-on experience with faith reflection, to name just a few.

A separate set of resources, all appearing under the title *Welcome to Christ* (see list of resources at the back of this book), has already been published for working with adult candidates who have not been baptized (people the church has traditionally called "catechumens"). The full range of resources in this book may not be needed for active members of other congregations who wish to transfer their membership into a new congregation. Such persons may benefit from a process of incorporation into membership that culminates in baptismal affirmation, however, and they should be given the opportunity to take part in this kind of ministry.

May the word and sacrament ministry of each of our congregations do no less than the bell from one Wisconsin church did:

> To the bath and the table,
> To the prayers and the word,
> I call every seeking soul.[1]

1. In *Holy Things: A Liturgical Theology* (Minneapolis: Fortress Press, 1993), Gordon Lathrop quotes from the inscription of a church bell that formerly served West Denmark Lutheran Church in Luck, Wisconsin.

Chapter 2

The Lure of Express Conversion

Then the prophet Jeremiah spoke to the prophet Hananiah in the presence of the priests and all the people who were standing in the house of the Lord *(Jeremiah 28:5).*

Long ago, two prophets stood up in the temple in Jerusalem at the dawn of the Babylonian exile and delivered two very different sermons (see Jeremiah 28:1-17). One was a bogus prophet. The other was the real thing. One spoke lies. The other spoke truth. But it was tough to tell the difference.

Hananiah prophesied that the exile would be brief. Speaking for God he boldly said, "Within two years I will bring back...all the exiles from Judah who went to Babylon" (28:3-4). It was a great sermon. People loved it. "Amens" were heard all around. He probably even got several nice compliments that day at the door. Hananiah's congregation was quite eager to sign up for the "express exile."

Jeremiah offered another sermon that day. In that same worship service, Jeremiah showed up with a wooden yoke around his neck and told the truth. God's people who were exiled to Babylon would remain not two years but *seventy* years. You may recall that Hananiah gets so mad that he grabs the yoke from Jeremiah's neck and smashes it to smithereens.

Hananiah preached the short cut. He was quite popular. "The exile is a minor inconvenience," he said. "Just a little divine turbulence. Nothing to worry about." People loved hearing about the easy way. They wanted to believe Hananiah's words, but he was wrong. Jeremiah told the truth. And the truth involved taking the long way—with no short cuts.

In an age of instant everything and quick gratification, it is very tempting for churches to offer newcomers an express route to membership—the shorter inconvenience touted by Hananiah. We do not like hearing that listening for God's word may take some effort and time—even a long time. Congregational council leaders may not see the need for quality adult education for new members, and may want an evangelism program that makes church life as accessible and trouble-free as possible. Many joining the church may want theological short cuts to membership and assimilation into Christ's body.

A recent phenomenon seems to be the popularity of books containing the word "little" in the title, such as *God's Little Instruction Book on Prayer, God's Little Devotional Book for Couples, God's Little Instruction Book on Success,* and even *God's Little Devotional Bible.* The clear message these titles convey is that God is both diminutive and manageable. Hananiah lives! We want the short cut. And when presented with that option we will usually take it.

Because you are reading a book about a new membership process, it is quite likely that you already know there is nothing "little" about the Christian life. There are no quick fixes for congregations seeking what Gordon Cosby calls "membership integrity."[1] Christianity is not a religion where a "little dab will do ya." Church leaders also realize that being so forthcoming with prospective members in an era of "church-shopping" may send a seeker down the street a few blocks where the membership expectations do not seem so rigid. Pastors are sorely tempted to offer a hurried, watered-down, express version of Christian initiation, which we justify in a thousand different ways.

The truth is that we are doing inquirers a great disservice when we rush them into membership. Conversion, contrary to popular perception, is not a moment in time. "I was addicted to QVC, Mounds Bars, and Oprah, but now I've found Jesus and everything is instantly better." No. It takes *time* to discern exactly what is at stake when one commits to follow Jesus. As Daniel Berrigan once stated, a Christian should be prepared to look good on wood. An inquirer needs plenty of room to "estimate the cost" of following Jesus prior to baptism or affirmation of baptism (Luke 14:28). Rushing the process in the name of "inclusion" with a person who is brand-new to church life has consistently led to membership *inactivity*. Frequently inquirers have never been given the opportunity to see how Jesus calls people to a life that is often at great odds with the dominant culture. True faith and life in Christ have not always been fully explored in the new member process.

Several years ago a man called "Henry" showed up at worship for the first time in thirty years and sat near the back of a church. Henry, who that fall entered a process leading to re-affirmation of his baptism, later wrote these reflections about his return to church.

> I grew up in the Southern Baptist tradition or lack thereof. I gradually drifted from my parents and church because I couldn't rectify the dogmatic gaps in the Baptist faith with the tools of mind-body-spirit that I had been culturally endowed with. I rebelled, turned to drugs, rock 'n' roll, esoteric mysticism, and chugged huge cut-glass pitchers of cheap grace. I reconsidered the church at this juncture the way a person in a small rowboat approaching Niagara Falls might consider an island protruding upward into his clandestine path.[2]

It does not take much pastoral intuition to perceive that Henry needed much more than a short series of sessions leading to church membership. He would not be part of a faith community today if the congregation he approached had not taken his needs seriously. In these few sentences, Henry reveals several issues common to many people who return to church after a long absence.

Alienation from a childhood church

Congregations often welcome many people who arrive with a warped image of God from a damaging religious past. Many people leave church at a young age for very clear reasons, including emotional survival.[3] Barbara Brown Taylor quotes a mother who defends her daughter's ignorance of Christianity, "My daughter doesn't know Moses from Goliath but at least she grew up without guilt."[4] Early perceptions of God are powerful and lasting and should not be dismissed in a newcomer's first few months back to church.

The emptiness of an undisciplined life without God

Henry came to a church because the culture he had so eagerly embraced as an alternative to church left him empty and without purpose or meaning. Any true conversion must honestly address not only what a person is taking on in turning to Christ, but also what one is leaving behind. According to the late Jim Dunning, an early pioneer of the *Rite of Christian Initiation of Adults* (RCIA) in the Roman Catholic church, this includes "not [simply] bringing God to people but helping them discern a presence that has always been."[5] God was at work in Henry's life, even though he had been away from a congregation for many years.

A return to church out of desperation as well as hope

One of our assumptions in ministry to inquiring adults is that they arrive either in transition or crisis. Very few people seek out a congregation just to admire its lovely sanctuary. God brings them. A smart congregation will help a seeker find out why God has done that. An effective ministry with inquirers assumes that God calls each baptized person into exciting and unique endeavors for the sake of Christ.

Conversion to Christ and life in his body—the church—can never be a rushed process. Death and new life are at work. As William Willimon has written:

> When you join Rotary they give you a handshake and a lapel pin. When you join the church we throw you in the water and half drown you. Ponder that. Whatever signing on with Jesus means, it means that we will not do just as we are, that change is demanded, daily, sometimes painful turning and detoxification that does not come naturally.[6]

Henry's baptismal affirmation at the Easter Vigil several years ago was joyful and liberating, but he would also claim that it was painful getting there. Nothing less than the full death and resurrection of Christ was at work in him. True conversion always involves both shadow and light. A caring congregation that fully welcomes a newcomer into new life in Christ must devote itself to both elements.

It is important for all congregational leaders to understand that adult newcomers need much more than many congregations have traditionally offered. Sometimes it is easy to be swayed by the voice of Hananiah in congregational life. Things seem to be going so well. We dress up for church, flash our best Sunday smile at the ushers, and keep our distance from God. It is easy to fool people. Perhaps those who are not easily fooled are the ones returning to church, looking for an authentic alternative to the emptiness of a fast-food culture long on promises and short on spiritually nourishing food.

The Church As Counter-Cultural Story

> *Were not our hearts burning within us while he was talking to us on the road, while he was opening the scriptures to us? (Luke 24:32).*

It is getting dark. Two men approach the town limits in a slow, shuffling sort of way that reveals they have more on their minds than a warm bed and a hot meal. There is something bothering them. Can you see it? They look like they've just come from a funeral of a good friend. They keep walking, heads down, occasionally talking in low tones. One of them goes by the name of Cleopas—the only time he's ever mentioned in the Bible. The other is unnamed. We are invited to walk along with them.

Notice: they are walking *away* from Jerusalem. Seven miles separate them now from their old friends who still wait in the city and dare to hope. As far as we can tell, these two have given up on their old community of friends. They have given up on Jesus and on what would soon become the early church. They are walking the other way. Yet we will not judge them negatively for the direction they take. Our own faith ebbs and flows as theirs does. Walking the other way—away from the community, away from Jerusalem towards Emmaus—is a very real and appealing possibility. Who has not thought of leaving the church at one time or another?

The two men walking toward Emmaus tell the stranger on the road, "We had hoped that he was the one to redeem Israel." *Had hoped.* Their eyes are wide open now. Jesus is dead. It is time to head home and be grown-ups about their disappointment.

In his book *How to Reach Secular People*, George Hunter claims that about one-third of secular, unchurched people are what he calls "ignostics," people who have "no Christian memory" and "don't know what Christians are talking about."[7] Many people seeking the church these days do have *some* Christian memory (like Henry from the preceding section) and can usually recall a Cleopas-like experience that led them away from the church. Jesus was no longer real for them. They wanted to believe, but could not intellectually find common ground between basic scientific facts and the perceived fictions of the Bible. In their minds the Bible was a storybook they had simply outgrown.

In John Updike's novel *In the Beauty of the Lilies*, Clarence Wilmot is the pastor of Fourth Presbyterian Church in Paterson, New Jersey. He wakes up one morning in the year 1910 with an overwhelming feeling of "God's inexorable recession." Clarence has been fighting feelings of doubt for some time since reading a controversial book called *Some Mistakes of Moses* and finally decides to resign his call and sell encyclopedias door-to-door. He concludes that he is much more comfortable with certainty than speculation, so he sells these books of facts instead. In his novel, Updike says a lot about our culture's need for information and getting the facts straight. So many inquirers feel what Cleopas felt on that road so long ago. The facts were painfully clear. "We had hoped but..." There is nothing quite so devastating as hope once cherished now lost. Better to trust facts only. Many people returning to church are reopening an old can of worms they thought was permanently closed.

To trust the Bible in an era where facts hold so much authority is a supreme countercultural exercise. Recall Exodus 14. There the Egyptians are in hot pursuit of the children of God, tailing them all the way to the Red Sea. Waters part. Israel is saved. And then we encounter this grisly scene even Disney couldn't soften in *The Prince of Egypt*: "The waters returned and covered the chariots and the chariot drivers, the entire army of Pharaoh that had followed them into the sea; not one of them remained" (14:28). Not one? *Titanic* looks tame in comparison. Postmodern seekers cringe at stories like these. This was the God they had fled long ago. "What kind of God is this?" they ask. "And I thought the Noah story was confusing. Enough with the water. What kind of God drowns people?"

Modern people often approach the Bible in one of two ways. 1) We worship the book (instead of the God to whom the book points) and try to make literal, word-for-word sense out of every jot and tittle, or 2) We disregard the book entirely, leaving its stories in the nursery of our childhoods, having now "outgrown" such elementary fictions, opting instead for rigid fact and scientific certainty.

What would happen if we read Exodus 14 through a baptismal lens instead? What difference would it make if we read the Egyptian carnage as a foreshadowing of sin's hot pursuit and God's sacramental drowning in the watery event of our rebirth in Christ? It is a powerful revelation for seekers to discover that the Bible's truth is revealed in story and symbol and poetry much more than in an assemblage of wooden facts. In an age of information, we all need a larger story, a bigger canvas, a more honest mirror in which to make sense of our lives. So the Bible tells stories of giants, floods, scoundrels, exiles, prodigals, dreams, jailbreaks, and earthquakes. We find our stories in that wider story. They leave us breathless and spent, now dependent on the God who breathes new life into old bones and washes the church up on a Red Sea shore, alive.

What makes Cleopas and his companion hike back to town excitedly even after sundown? These same two men—at first moving away from Jerusalem, away from the community, away from church—now race back towards all three. It is dark now and they decide to walk the seven miles anyway. The two look at one another just before setting off and say, "Were not our hearts burning within us while he was talking to us on the road, while he was *opening the scriptures* to us?" (Luke 24:32).

"Christians," says Eugene Peterson, "do not simply learn or study or use Scripture; we assimilate it, take it into our lives in such a way that it gets metabolized into acts of love, cups of cold water, missions into all the world, healing and evangelism and justice in Jesus' name, hands raised in adoration of the Father."[8] There are few things more important than helping inquirers mired in a culture of facts to find their true identity not in more information, but rather in a story that forms new lives. The Bible opens the canvas of our lives to possibilities beyond the purely factual. More than one inquirer has described a rediscovery of the Bible as a journey into a whole new land, akin to stepping through the wardrobe into Narnia. A feast of stories in the Bible wait to form new disciples, set hearts burning, and open once-hopeless eyes to the reality of the risen Christ.

Baptized into Our Worst Fears

> *So the sisters sent a message to Jesus, "Lord, he whom you love is ill." But when Jesus heard it, he said, "This illness does not lead to death" (John 11:3-4a).*

When conversion is allowed to unfold over time, giving the counter-cultural stories of the Bible room to work and take root in a person's life, something very much like death begins to occur in a person. "Do you not know that all of us who have been baptized into Christ Jesus were baptized into his death?" (Romans 6:3). That may just be the most unnerving question in the entire Bible. During Lent, people on the journey of faith are encouraged to ask, "What is dying in my life? What am I leaving behind?" Because we live in a culture absolutely paralyzed by the fear of death, these questions create no small amount of tension in the life of a person new to church life.

It is curious how Jesus responds with such seeming nonchalance to two very worried sisters who send him word about their sick brother Lazarus. "This illness does not lead to death." Talk about a classic misdiagnosis! Jesus is alarmingly laid back about this news. The author of the story takes special pains to tell us that, after hearing about Lazarus's poor health, Jesus "stayed two days longer in the place where he was" (John 11:6). No need to interrupt his plans. "This illness does not lead to death."

Well, what would you call it? Is Lazarus just dressing up like a mummy for Halloween later in the story? Before they roll away the stone at the tomb, practical Martha says, "Lord, he's been dead four days. It'll smell to high heaven in there." We all know that Lazarus is deader than a doornail, but

Jesus says, "Don't worry. You cannot die from this."

When Jesus finally does arrive in Bethany (the name of the town literally means "House of Affliction"), each sister in turn runs out and says the same thing. "Lord, if you had been here my brother would not have died." Perhaps they really said something like, "Where have you *been*, anyway, Jesus? If you had gotten off your rear end, our brother would still be around." Can we forgive Jesus for a misdiagnosis? Can we give him a break? He makes it right in the end, doesn't he?

It is interesting that in John's gospel Jesus never once grumbles about his destiny or complains about dying; no request that the cup might be taken away; no cry of dereliction from the cross. He even carries it himself. Jesus seems to be aware of another reality that death cannot touch, so he is able to play around with his life and take risks that amaze us. He is not pulled this way and that by death threats. He does not go to Lazarus's side right away. He is not jerked around by physical death.

What seems to bother Jesus is spiritual death—in which people become so obsessed with dying that they never truly live. "For those who want to save their life will lose it." "Unbind him, let him go," Jesus says to the community that has entombed Lazarus. Surrounded by the best medical care, state-of-the-art security devices, and insurance policies that cover every mishap, we are still so very fearful and bound by the reality of death. We are busy saving and protecting our lives.

Think of the loveable Garp in John Irving's classic book *The World According to Garp*, who is a paranoid dad convinced that every screeching tire in his neighborhood is a potential menace to his children. So he wears running shoes all the time and chases down speeders on foot. "Sometimes, if the car was going really fast, Garp would need three or four stop signs to catch up to it. Once he sprinted five blocks and was so out of breath when he caught up to the offending car that the driver was sure there'd been a murder in the neighborhood and Garp was either trying to report it or had done it himself."[9] Garp knew. There are bad things that can "get us" out there. We can worry so much about the bad things that we are bound by the worry. Martha and Mary knew about the bad things, too. They knew what could happen to loved ones. That is why they desperately called Jesus. "This illness does not lead to death," he said. In other words, according to Jesus, the bad things we think can "get us" *truly can't*. But there are worse things that can. We can die spiritually—from caution and fear and lack of trust. In Jesus' diagnostic mind, this is the real illness that *does* lead to death. Jesus was speaking to Lazarus that day but he could just as easily have been speaking to our culture: "Unbind them, let them go."

Built in to every aspect of a person's coming to faith is an overarching sacramental invitation to pattern one's life after the death and resurrection of Jesus. It is impossible to be a participant in the process without having one's nose rubbed in death almost every step of the way. "Do you not know that all of us who have been baptized into Christ Jesus were baptized into his death?" (Romans 6:3).

If we are honest, the world is one big "house of affliction." Our culture desperately needs many places and ways to talk about our fear of death and how we might overcome that fear through faith and trust in Christ. Jesus does not shield us from suffering and death. If we watch him closely, follow him, and learn from him, he will keep us from something far worse. He will keep us from an unhealthy dread of the grave—an illness that leads to death before we die. The church offers a wonderful gift to a world so bound. Having *already* died in baptism, we are free to confront physical death and begin living into the gift of resurrection now. "I *am* the resurrection and the life," Jesus says to a grieving sister (John 11:25). Present tense.

Following the Resurrected Christ in a Culture of Disbelief

> *Jesus said to Mary, "Do not hold on to me, because I have not yet ascended to the Father" (John 20:17a).*

In John's account of Easter morning everybody is surely flying down a path. Mary goes to the tomb, finds it empty, and starts running. Peter and another disciple hear the news and off they go. The men even seem to race against each other in the dark.

Back and forth poor Mary runs. "They have taken the Lord!" The men look in. One believes. Both go back to bed, but not Mary. She stays and weeps. The details just do not add up. These little bits of peek-a-boo evidence provide only hints. Here. Gone. Here. Gone. Missing body. Folded graveclothes. Couple of angels. Only the gardener. Here a glimpse. There a glimpse. Here. Gone.

Why doesn't Jesus show himself? Why isn't Easter more obvious and clear for Mary? For all those returning to our churches looking for Jesus, wouldn't it be a lot easier if Jesus did not seem so veiled and hidden? Most maddening is that moment when Mary finally recognizes Jesus. If this were a Hollywood version, Mary and Jesus would be dancing circles in a field of tulips, monarch butterflies would gently flap in the wind, Barry Manilow would sing in the background, and all the neighborhood children would find golden eggs hidden in the grass.

Remember what Jesus says to Mary just after she finally figures out who is standing in front of her. Mary presumably goes to hug Jesus and he says, "Do not hold on to me, because I have not yet ascended to my Father." It is hard to imagine Jesus not hugging somebody but he says right out, "Don't touch me. Hands off. Don't even think about touching me."

There have been various attempts to try and make sense of such mysterious behavior. A likely explanation is that Jesus is trying to tell Mary that he will not be around anymore in the way that he once was. Things have changed. "Don't hold on to me." There is a side of us that wants Jesus to come back and appear on *60 Minutes* so that everybody, especially the unbelievers within each of us, can be absolutely sure. "Tell us how it was when you were dead, sir," Mike Wallace would say.

But about the best we can hope for, this side of the grave, are glimpses of Jesus alive inside our lives. Flashes of divine insight, fleeting as a firefly. Here. Gone. As the apostle Paul once put it, "Now we see in a mirror, dimly, but then we will see face to face. Now I know only in part; then I will know fully, even as I have been fully known" (1 Corinthians 13:12). Now dimly. Now in part. Such is the nature of Easter.

This may unnerve not a few seekers of Christ who wish to be certain and "have proof" prior to embarking on the way of discipleship. The church itself may be part of the problem in that, while we are called to be stewards of the mysteries of Easter, an unfortunate air of authority and certainty often colors our public pronouncements. Richard Rohr states:

> Religion has not tended to create seekers or searchers, has not tended to create honest humble people who trust that God is always beyond them. We aren't focused on the great mystery. Religion has, rather, tended to create people who think they have God in their pockets, people with quick, easy, glib answers.[10]

A letter to an avowed atheist recently touched on "God's unmerited gifts of grace" that fall into the laps of believer and unbeliever alike. The friend wrote back in part:

> One thing you could answer. Would you name [an unmerited gift] so I'll know what you are talking about? And explain how it is unmerited. And does this imply that some gifts are merited? Or is nothing in life merited? 'God's benevolent gifts' is an extreme absurdity to me. Most of us could understand God granting life benevolently—we hugely respect life. But within the confines of life, God seems to have let chance rule. If you get too specific regarding God's responsibility, God seems equal part monster and benevolent father. [In the spring 1999 school shootings] at Littleton, Colorado the young man with the gun [purportedly] said to the blond young girl, 'Do you believe in God?' She said 'yes' and was shot to death. Was that merited? Unmerited?

This friend is not unique. He and many others—people actually giving church a second look—are not searching for "quick, easy, glib answers." Our task then, as church leaders, is not to tidy up the faith and make it palatable for a disbelieving culture, removing all mystery. Instead, we are called to *deepen* the mystery of God and not try to explain away the absurdities ("foolishness," says Paul, in 1 Corinthians 1:18-25) of faith in Christ. Perhaps the greatest gift we can give to an inquirer is to place that person within the context of tradition and the church year, giving the Spirit time and space to brood over and groan with someone who brings articulate, if painful, questions to the whole enterprise of faith. As Luther said in his explanation to the third article of the Apostles' Creed, even faith is ultimately a gift of the Spirit. We never try to orchestrate, manipulate, or rush such a gift.

> The vast majority of people are sitting in the pews with parched lips. They are so thirsty that they have lost their ability to listen, to speak, or to think. But one big gulp of Gatorade is not the answer. They will drown. Their thirst is so great that it requires a series of sips much like parched fields require a series of gentle rains.[11]

Summary

This chapter has highlighted four cultural challenges for church leaders who work with unbaptized adults, seekers returning to church after an absence of some time, or members within the parish setting who wish to deepen their discipleship.

- The very real lure of express conversion in an era of instant everything
- Developing a love for biblical story in a culture of fact-finding
- Sacramental immersion in the death of Jesus so that physical death loses its hold
- Deepening the mystery of Jesus, who is always beyond us, drawing us forward

These challenges, of course, are not exhaustive but seem to be recurring issues brought by the many interesting people who have entered church life as adult inquirers. What is certainly true is that we cannot continue to welcome adults into the church as we might have half a century ago. A culture once overwhelmingly Christian in America now lists affiliation with a church as one spiritual option among many. Pastors can no longer assume a "cradle to grave" affiliation with a congregation. Christ's church is in a period of important and critical change.

Tertullian once said, "Disciples are made, not born." The process that will be unfolded in the following chapters offers a time-tested model of making disciples in a pluralistic culture. The process offers ample opportunity to address directly the four challenges listed above. But above all, it joyfully resurrects an old word whose language we have lost: conversion. Conversion to Christ is, of course, always unfinished business with a disciple. But for a church wishing to take evangelism seriously in a culture with a variety of challenges, here is a wonderful place to begin.

---

1. Cosby is long-time pastor of Church of the Saviour in Washington, D.C. The church requires a two-year period of reflection and study prior to membership. All members annually commit to a covenant that reads in part: "I unreservedly and with abandon commit my life and destiny to Christ, promising to give him a practical priority in all the affairs of life . . . regardless of the expenditures of time, energy and money." Cosby is convinced that one cannot come to make such a statement sincerely without a wholesale restructuring of how most congregations welcome new members.

2. This is an unpublished reflection written by a member of the author's congregation.

3. See especially Barbara Kingsolver's *The Poisonwood Bible* (HarperFlamingo, 1998) and Sheri Reynolds' *The Rapture of Canaan* (Berkley Books, 1995). The popularity of these novels is attributable in some degree to the very clear first-person voice given to women who are products of an abusive religious past.

4. Barbara Brown Taylor, *The Preaching Life* (Cambridge, Mass.: Cowley Publications, 1993).

5. James B. Dunning, *New Wine: New Wineskins, Exploring the RCIA* (New York: William H. Sadlier, Inc., 1981), 29.

6. William H. Willimon, *Peculiar Speech: Preaching to the Baptized* (Grand Rapids, Mich.: Wm. B. Eerdmans Publishing Co., 1992), 32.

7. George G. Hunter, III, *How to Reach Secular People* (Nashville: Abingdon Press, 1992), 41.

8. Eugene Peterson, "Eat This Book: The Holy Community at Table with the Holy Scripture," *Theology Today* (April 1999), 6.

9. John Irving, *The World According to Garp* (New York: Pocket Books, 1976), 254.

10. Richard Rohr, *Everything Belongs: The Gift of Contemplative Prayer* (New York: The Crossroad Publishing Company, 1999), 33.

11. Barbara Brown Taylor, *When God Is Silent* (Boston: Cowley Publications, 1998), 85-86. The author of this quote is an anonymous friend of Taylor's suggesting a model for preaching. The image of a "series of sips" also works as a model for Christian formation in a catechumenal setting.

Chapter 3

Movements and Moments on the Way to Affirmation of Baptism

The journey of faith in the body of Christ is one of gradual and continuous movement. When significant transitions like baptism are celebrated or affirmed, the tendency is to focus on the outer event itself, while less attention may be given to the interior and reflective processes preceding and following the celebration.

In the process of coming to faith or identifying with a Christian congregation, there are various transitional points that can serve as significant opportunities for intentional ministry and celebration within the Christian community. Recent studies of both the World Council of Churches and the Lutheran World Federation affirm baptism as having both inner movements and an outer rite. A statement from the World Council affirms that baptism is a "*process* and once-for-all eschatological *event* and *pattern* for all of life."[1] A process for approaching baptism or the affirmation of baptism asks that congregations do justice to both of these dimensions of baptism as they welcome new members to the life of faith in Christ.

In Luther's explanation of the third article of the Apostles' Creed we may see the movement to deepened conversion and baptismal living.

> I believe that by my own understanding or strength I cannot believe in Jesus Christ my Lord or come to him, but instead the Holy Spirit has called me through the gospel, enlightened me with his gifts, made me holy, and kept me in the true faith, just as he calls, gathers, enlightens, and makes holy the whole Christian church on earth and keeps it with Jesus Christ in the one common, true faith.[2]

The calling, gathering, enlightening, and making holy movements are a helpful summation of an ancient process known as the catechumenate. Gordon Lathrop has explored how the root structure of baptism is scriptural, a structure which he calls "the great pattern of baptizing."[3]

This fourfold pattern reflects natural human times or periods of conversion. New members move from the first movement of questioning or longing to the second movement of reading scripture and experiencing the faith, to the third movement of developing a prayer life and preparing for baptism or the affirmation of baptism, and to the fourth movement of living the baptized life. There are a variety of terms for these four times, as well as sets of prayers or liturgical rites that may be used to mark the transitions from one time to the next. But this fourfold pattern has been recognized as the most helpful basic shape for describing how people prepare to become a part of a Christian community.

Some have likened entry into God's household as a progression from the front porch to the living room, then the dining room, and finally the family room. Each room symbolizes a different level of human intimacy. Still others have described growth in faith more like the development of human relationships. Vincent Peterson describes the entry into the household of faith like the transitions that precede and accompany marriage.[4] He lists the four states as: (a) Getting Acquainted—acceptance, friendship, and self-revelation, (b) Making a Decision—dating, desiring to know the loved one, and announcing an engagement, (c) Deepening the Commitment—accepting, affirming, and forgiving one another during the engagement and during the marriage itself, and (d) Celebrating the Gift—from the honeymoon through all the years of living together as a couple.

Questions and Stories: The Time of Inquiry

The first movement of a journey to affirmation of baptism allows inquirers to decide if they want to explore the Christian faith further. Those who facilitate the time of inquiry—whether lay catechists or clergy—encourage inquirers to be attentive to the call of God. Inquirers are also assigned sponsors from the congregation, who usually attend meetings and worship with them.

During inquiry, questions and experiences need to be explored. This is the time for raising the primary questions, or what John Smith terms the "ultimate questions": Where have I come from? What is the goal and destiny of life? What am I responsible for and what is of value?[5] Abraham Maslow explains that these "age-old 'spiritual' questions" are the perennial human questions of meaning, belonging, suffering, and death. He frames them in this way:

> What is the good life? What is the good man? The good woman? What is the good society and what is my relation to it? What are my obligations to society? What is best for my children? What is justice? Truth? Virtue? What is my relation to nature, to death, to aging, to pain, to illness? How can I live a zestful, enjoyable, meaningful life? What is my responsibility to my brothers [and sisters]? Who *are* my brothers [and sisters]? What shall I be loyal to? What must I be ready to die for?[6]

For some inquirers it will take considerable time to address certain questions and to move through them. It is important for inquirers to see that no question is irrelevant or irreverent. Constraints of time and the dynamics of a new member group should never prevent questions from being raised.

Many congregations have learned that persons with little or no previous church background may best be served with an inquiry process of their own apart from other affirmers who are more experienced members of the church. The reason is simple. Total newcomers to the church frequently have different needs and questions than people who have already become familiar with Bible stories and basic Christian practices. There may be exceptions to this guideline, but it can be helpful to keep in mind. A group composed mostly of "advanced" inquirers can crowd out the more basic questions of those new to Christian faith—and may in extreme cases appear threatening or even hostile to the inexperienced newcomer.

The heart of the time of inquiry is storytelling. Inquirers will have stories that speak of critical turning points in their journeys of faith. These stories of life experiences reveal inquirers wrestling with issues around loss, illness, or death as well as celebrating achievement, love, or birth. The skilled leader will help connect these stories to the stories of scripture. Personal images of desert or mountaintop experiences will become entry points for great stories of the faith. Inquirers will come to see their own stories having parallels in the stories of scripture.

The length of this time for inquiry varies with the people involved. It is important that the time of inquiry not be rushed according to a preset pattern. The leader of an inquirer's group, along with the sponsors involved, needs to be sensitive to the time frame of the work of the Spirit and to the individual inquirer's response. Some people may decide even after a few brief conversations that they are not yet ready to commit to a time of study and discernment of the Spirit's presence in their lives. If this is the case, the inquiry time will still have done its work. It will have helped people determine whether or not they are ready for the Christian life.

Inquirers who are ready to proceed further may be readied to participate in a service of welcome. This liturgical order (see Welcome of Inquirers for Affirmation of Baptism, appendix F, p. 81) recognizes where the inquirers are in their faith development and allows them to express God's movement in their lives. The inquirers' experiences up to this point may have been primarily with other individuals and in a small group. In the order of welcome they will be opened to the grace that is present in a regular worship service of the congregation. While such a service of worship along the way to the affirmation of baptism serves as a transition time marking a movement in the life and commitment of the inquirer, it is also important for the congregation to assert its willingness to be the new home for these people. This public order of worship itself may open inquirers to a deeper awareness of God's grace and to a deeper connectedness to the congregation.

The questions to be asked of the inquirers before the congregation will be:

- What do you ask of God's church?
- What do you seek from God's Word?[7]

Among the questions the inquirers may have been pondering and praying about privately and in the inquiry group are ones like the following: "Do I feel that God is working in Jesus, reconciling the world [to God]? Do I feel that Christ can be known and experienced in the various sacraments?"[8] The order of welcome asks the inquirers if they are committed to finding out about the faith. Actions of signing with the cross and of blessing accompany prayers for the inquirers to encounter Christ and be renewed by the Spirit.

Experiencing Church: Towards Affirmation

Following the welcome from the congregation, those preparing for affirmation of baptism typically gather with their sponsors and a guide (or leader) weekly—often after a worship service of the congregation. This movement may begin at any time throughout the year. The intent of instruction during this second movement or time is not ultimately for information about God, but for transformation into the way of Christ.

During this second movement those preparing for affirmation of baptism begin to experience Christian community. This is the time for encountering Christ's presence in the church. Andrew Parker, in writing of the immersion into Christ's way, makes clear the need of both the new member group and the entire parish in this ministry:

> Being formed as a Christian is too important (literally, too crucial) to leave to a single individual teaching a six-week class. The promises which we make in baptism and reaffirm in confirmation and regularly thereafter are solemn, profound, and demanding. Learning how to immerse yourself in the apostles' teaching and fellowship, the breaking of bread, and the prayers, how to persevere in resisting evil, how to repent, how to proclaim in word and example the good news of God

> in Christ, how to seek and serve Christ in all persons and how to strive for justice and peace among all people…It takes deep and sustained reflection, discipline, and prayer. It takes a whole community of people, with their profuse variety of gifts and temperaments, who are willing to walk with you and support you along the way.[9]

This second movement incorporates the major elements of being church: reading scripture, prayer, worship, and ministry in daily life. Through these four elements, affirmers experience the full range of what the church does when it gathers.

Reading scripture

Weekly scripture reflection ordinarily extends from Sunday's scripture readings (or lectionary). Exploration of these weekly scripture readings helps persons explore the central teachings of Christianity and deepen their growth in God's grace. This is now time to come to know, internalize, and apply the word. The word *catechesis* means the "echoing" of the word of God in one's life and for the world. As James Dunning has written, "We ground evangelization/catechesis in the word of God and that makes some of the best scholarly conversation with that word more accessible so that it echoes, reverberates and literally resounds in our times."[10] This "echoing" of the word opens the dialogue between the lives of affirmers and Christ. The place of scripture is central to catechesis because it incarnates Christ to human beings.

Prayer

A second element of the experience of church is prayer. Formation of people in the spirit and life of prayer is an important part of their preparation for membership in the body of Christ. In baptism Christians become part of a people who practice a life of prayer. The catechist will be sensitive to the regular and spontaneous rhythms of the need of prayer within the group. In addition to an opening and closing prayer in small group gatherings, the leader may invite time for prayer in the midst of a second or third reading of a scripture text or at some poignant moment in the group's faith sharing. Opportunities are provided to talk together about approaches to prayer and differences in prayer styles. Prayers can also be nurtured in the ways the scriptures are read. A wide range of prayer methods can be used for meditation and to listen and respond to scripture.

Worship in the assembly

A third element of the experience of church is weekly worship of the congregation. A small group might often meet on Sundays, which may be helpful in bringing together public worship and catechesis. It is chiefly through the experience of public worship that people are brought into the body of Christ. Gordon Lathrop writes of the importance of worship and catechesis being interrelated: "…the Christian meeting, in all its signs and words, says something authentic and reliable about God, and so says something true about ourselves and about our world as they are understood before God."[11] Small group guides (or leaders) help persons preparing for affirmation of baptism to prepare for the worship of the congregation, and facilitate reflection and action following the celebrations. Having sponsors who can guide inquirers through a congregation's worship is an important part of the total experience—it is quite simply an experience of hospitality.

Ministry in daily life

A fourth critical dimension of the church's life for affirmers to experience is that of service. Persons preparing for affirmation of baptism may be invited to observe and participate in a congregation's service events, perhaps alongside their sponsors. It is also possible that those who are preparing for affirmation of baptism may already be involved in a social ministry of some kind—living out one's faith in the business world, in a hospice ministry, through a tutoring program, or in a ministry to refugees. Whatever the experiences, it is important that this part of the Christian life not be neglected in a critical period of formation for a Christian. From these experiences that are guided through the ministry of a small group, affirmers are invited into service at both personal and communal levels. As the group reflects on what may have happened to them throughout a week or what seems to be going on in a scripture text, they are invited to understand their own lives in relationship to where they are being called to love and serve God.

Like the first movement, the second movement has no ideal or prescribed length. It needs to be long enough for those preparing for affirmation of baptism to have discovered some of the central truths of the Christian faith and to have become familiar with many of the central stories in the scriptures. This period of time may be from several weeks to a year or more. The timing of this movement all depends on a person's readiness to enter the community of faith more fully. It may not be identical for everyone who has been a part of the same small group. Has an affirmer come to know Christ? Does she have a basic understanding of Christian teachings and patterns of life? While each person of faith always has more to learn and to experience, there comes a point at which people are ready to enter the Christian community more fully and to begin to prepare for that day more intensively.

Many congregations receive candidates for baptism during the season of Lent (sometimes Advent, as well). The candidates and their sponsors may gather with the congregation at the beginning of Lent for a time of enrollment—actually signing their intention to prepare themselves for baptism.[12] Those who are preparing for affirmation of baptism may also be brought before the congregation at or near this time. The intention is to focus the prayers of the congregation around the candidates in the final weeks of their preparation.

Baptismal Preparation: Time of Preparation

The third movement in the journey, that of baptismal preparation, is a time for candidates to enter more deeply into the faith of the church, into a life of personal and communal prayer, and into reflection on the life of dying and rising in Christ. While reflection on one's life has been part of the process already, it becomes even more intentional for the candidates during Lent (or the alternate time of Advent). Often congregations have special ways of renewing their own baptismal commitments during the season of Lent. The candidates' preparation for affirmation of baptism will be strengthened in being part of a congregation that is aware of the need for daily repentance and conversion.

All three movements to this point have been focused on directing the candidates to claiming, forming, and articulating a personal faith in God, as well as growing to affirm the creeds of the church. The candidates are nurtured in such a way that they gain confidence in articulating their own faith. Images and stories that have been told along the way to the affirmation of baptism help them to celebrate how God has touched their lives.

During this movement of preparation, candidates are invited to acquire a spirit of repentance and to desire forgiveness and healing. As the candidates acknowledge the reality of sin and separation from God, they consider the complexity of personal, impersonal, and societal sin. While they face their own sin and pray about their failures, they also reflect on systemic sins like consumerism, individualism, racism, sexism, as well as others.

The third movement of preparation encourages candidates to develop a life of prayer more intentionally. They will enter more deeply into the worship life of the congregation during this movement. Often the candidates might gather for a weekend retreat of prayer and reflection—perhaps in the final week or two preceding affirmation of baptism. Extended prayer sessions are important so that this time does not become overly focused on cognitive learning of doctrine. This may also be an appropriate opportunity to introduce people to the possibility of individual confession and forgiveness.

Questions to be asked of the candidates at affirmation of baptism quite naturally become a part of the third movement:

> I ask you to profess your faith in Christ Jesus, reject sin, and confess the faith of the Church....
>
> Do you renounce all the forces of evil, the devil, and all his empty promises?[13]

Affirmation of baptism is the most celebrative moment to which the candidates have been moving. Martin Luther made clear the importance of this event: "We should therefore do justice to its meaning and make baptism a true and complete sign of the thing it signifies."[14] All the time of preparation prior to this event, and indeed the nurturing that follows it, is an attempt to accord baptism its proper and rightful place.

When the affirmation of baptism occurs at the Easter Vigil, the church can employ all the rich baptismal symbols that are uniquely available to it through this liturgy. This liturgy allows for lavish use of the symbols of baptismal death and rebirth. Symbols of darkness, fire, word, cross, water, laying on of hands, oil, and the finest bread and wine, all serve to interpret what happens through baptism. Those who will affirm their baptism are accompanied by their sponsors during this entire service that culminates the movements of preparation. Scripture readings during the Easter Vigil are stories that sustain the faithful and speak of our common identity. Fundamentally they speak of both sinner and saved, about being strong in one's weakness, and about being made free from bondage.

Savoring and Serving: Baptismal Living

The fourth movement, traditionally a time of reflection on what has happened in the sacraments of baptism and communion, begins the ongoing time of baptismal living. Ideally, the newly affirmed continue to gather regularly for conversation, scripture reading, and prayer for some weeks following the Easter Vigil (throughout the fifty days of Easter, or throughout the Epiphany season if baptism took place on the Baptism of Our Lord). New members would continue to worship with their sponsors during the beginning of this final movement. It is unsound to expect new members, after an intimate and powerful small group faith experience, to enter a congregation where there are no occasions for faith sharing, storytelling, scripture study, and communal prayer. A serious life of discipleship can only be sustained by ongoing small group opportunities in the congregation in which people continue to gather for reading the scriptures, conversation, and prayer.

There are two dimensions during the fourth movement: the savoring of the sacramental experience and the baptismal call to service. The group assembles as usual the week following the affirmation of baptism, as close to the actual experience as possible. The small group leader who has been with the group during the time of preparation will encourage group members to be attentive to what happened within them during their experience of affirmation, and help them articulate that experience in words and images.

This reflection on the sacraments can only have personal depth if that discussion *follows* the actual experience. Maslow emphasizes how important it is to spend time in the savoring of experience. He writes: "Rituals, ceremonies, words, formulae may touch some, but they do not touch many unless their meanings have been deeply understood and experienced."[15] Luther emphasized how important it is for those who partake of the Lord's supper to be able to speak of its meaning and benefits.[16] Through the conversation about the two sacraments, the group leader will guide the newly baptized in seeing how the church understands the sacraments and why they are important as moments of grace that sustain faith.

In addition to savoring the grace of sacramental living, all Christians are called to live the sacraments for others and for the entire earth. Gordon Lathrop writes that, "The Christian arises from these waters to participation in the world-changing, witnessing, communal assembly around the Risen One, together with those who are in him."[17] While the entire baptismal initiation is aimed at forming a people for discipleship, all the baptized now take the time to find and take up a particular life of service. The movement toward putting one's baptism into practice will call the baptized into an even deeper realization of how much they still are called to change.

A number of questions will be explored as those who have affirmed baptism continue to discover their particular vocations within the Christian community and throughout their daily lives: How do I practice my baptism? Where do I find the cross in my life? How might I embody God's grace in the world? How can I be bread for the world? In what ways can I pour out my faith (love) for others in this coming week? Those having affirmed their baptism will assess and name their unique interests, gifts, and commitments. Such a discernment process may be aided by the use of inventories of spiritual gifts and individual spiritual direction.[18] A communal prayer life will sustain the newly affirmed in remaining open to how God continues to speak and transform their lives. This time in conversation and prayer is directed toward the finding, naming, and announcing of one's vocation in the world before the congregation.

The concern of the fourth movement is the mission of Christ's church and its common ministry as members of the priesthood of all believers. The exploration of discipleship is also supported through the congregation's preaching and worship during the Easter season.

On Pentecost (or the Transfiguration of Our Lord) the order of Affirmation of the Vocation of the Baptized in the World helps to proclaim the variety of gifts and ministries of every person. After communion, the recent affirmers and their sponsors gather at the font. After the prayers, they and their sponsors speak of their vocation in the world. One question will be asked of them before the congregation: "Will you endeavor to pattern your life on the Lord Jesus Christ, in gratitude to God and in service to one another?"[19]

This fourth and final movement is a lifelong and an unending time. The concrete tasks of love of neighbor and love of God to which Christians are called and to which their hearts are drawn are endlessly shifting. Growing to maturity in the baptized life is a continuous journey.

Adaptations for Those Affirming Baptism

The primary focus of the four movements described in this chapter were initially designed for the experience of those preparing for baptism. Frequently such persons have been named "catechumens." These basic fourfold movements may also apply to those preparing for affirmation of baptism, and so in this chapter we have imagined that baptized and unbaptized persons might experience a similar process. A word of caution though: persons who are preparing for affirmation of baptism are already members of the body of Christ. Their baptized status ought to make a difference in how they are received. For one thing, baptized persons are ordinarily already invited to receive communion—whether or not they have previously been received into the congregation or been confirmed. The baptized do not participate in liturgical services designed for persons preparing to be baptized (for instance, enrollment of candidates for baptism at the beginning of Lent). Orders of worship specifically designed for the preparation of candidates for affirmation have been included in appendix F–J of this volume (pp. 81–101). It should be obvious, though it bears repeating at this time, that no one, under any circumstance, is to be rebaptized. Baptism is once and for all time. If a person wishes to experience baptism anew, the appropriate vehicle for that is *affirmation* of baptism.

Another way to adapt the process outlined here is when affirmation of baptism occurs at a time other than Easter. A workable alternative might be for affirmation of baptism to occur at the Baptism of Our Lord (first Sunday after the Epiphany). Working backwards then, Calling of the Baptized to Continuing Conversion (see appendix G, p. 87) could happen on the first Sunday in Advent, with the order for welcome having been celebrated several weeks or months before that. Other alternatives are quite possible as well, though affirmation of baptism at the Easter Vigil may be most preferable. Traditional baptismal festivals are at the Easter Vigil, Pentecost Day (there could be a Pentecost vigil as well), All Saints Day (or the Sunday following), and the Baptism of Our Lord. Baptisms and affirmation of baptism might ordinarily be planned for these days on the congregation's calendar, even while exceptions to this plan could always be arranged.

---

1 "Becoming a Christian: The Ecumenical Implications of Our Common Baptism," *World Council of Churches Commission on Faith and Order Consultation,* FO/97: 13 Revised, 10.

2. Martin Luther, *A Contemporary Translation of Luther's Small Catechism,* trans. Timothy J. Wengert (Minneapolis: Augsburg Fortress, 1994), 29.

3. Gordon W. Lathrop, "Baptismal Ordo and Rites of Passage in the Church," *Baptism, Rites of Passage, and Culture* (Geneva: The Lutheran World Federation, 1999), 27–46.

4. Vincent Peterson, *Journey in Faith* (Los Angeles: Franciscan Communications, 1987).

5. John E. Smith, *Experience and God* (New York: Oxford University Press, 1968), 151.

6. Abraham H. Maslow, *Religions, Values, and Peak-Experiences* (New York: The Viking Press, 1970), 52.

7. See the order of welcome printed in appendix F, p. 81.

8. Raymond B. Kemp, *A Journey in Faith: An Experience of the Catechumenate* (New York: Sadler, 1979), 52.

9. Andrew D.Parker, "Would Someone Please Explain the Catechumenate?" *North American Association for the Catechumenate Newsletter* (August 1998).

10. James B. Dunning, *Echoing God's Word: Formation for Catechists and Homilists in a Catechumenal Church* (Arlington, Va: The North American Forum on the Catechumenate, 1993), xv.

11. Gordon W. Lathrop, *Holy Things: A Liturgical Theology* (Minneapolis: Fortress Press, 1993), 3.

12. "Enrollment of Candidates for Baptism," *Welcome to Christ: Lutheran Rites for the Catechumenate* (Minneapolis: Augsburg Fortress, 1997), 18–21.

13. *Lutheran Book of Worship* (Minneapolis: Augsburg Publishing House, 1978), 123.

14. Martin Luther, "The Holy and Blessed Sacrament of Baptism," *Word and Sacrament I,* vol. 35, *Luther's Works,* ed. E. Theodore Bachmann (Philadelphia: Muhlenberg Press, 1960), 29.

15. Maslow, 35.

16. Martin Luther, "An Order of Mass and Communion for the Church at Wittenberg 1523," *Liturgy and Hymns,* vol. 53, *Luther's Works,* ed. Ulrich S. Leupold (Philadelphia: Fortress Press, 1965), 32.

17. Lathrop, 35.

18. For an example of such resources see Jean Morris Trumbauer's *Sharing the Ministry* in the resource list on p. 112.

19. Affirmation of the Vocation of the Baptized in the World (see appendix J, p. 99).

Chapter 4

The Affirmers Small Group

"And the Spirit immediately drove him out into the wilderness" (Mark 1:12).

We do not travel in small groups anymore. Specifically, unrelated adult North Americans do not travel in functioning small groups of five to fifteen people. Technology and wealth have freed us from the necessity of relying on one another as we travel. The days of sharing hopes, anxieties, life stories, and dreams with cabin mates on a transatlantic crossing or with sleeper-car acquaintances on a transcontinental rail passage have been replaced by dozing a few hours on a jet or the enforced (and often cherished) isolation of solitary travel in a metal and glass bubble across monotonous interstate highways.

We are even further removed from an era (including all of recorded history prior to the twentieth century) when interaction with fellow travelers was not only a pleasant way to pass the time but was a necessity for survival, as in an ocean crossing on a sailing ship or a wilderness crossing in a caravan or wagon train. Yet it is this very situation—the condition of traveling through unfamiliar and sometimes perilous terrain with other adults who are unrelated and may be total strangers—that serves as an apt metaphor for the challenge facing adult inquirers as they contemplate the risks and rewards of becoming a part of a new congregational family.

The fact that there is scarce precedent for cooperative travel—geographical or spiritual—with strangers in our modern world is no small handicap to initiating a small group ministry for adult inquirers in a congregational setting. Our society has lost the presumption of trust in strangers, a reality that no doubt owes its existence to a lack of having to practice such trust. That the ecclesiastical world has resisted this trend away from small group travel (of the spiritual sort, as well as of the geographical sort), and has indeed nurtured and propagated small group ministry at many levels, is a helpful counter to the dearth of comparable secular precedents.

Before we consider adopting various congregational small group models for the ministry of welcoming adult inquirers, we must first acknowledge the special needs and expectations of adult inquirers, and then adjust these models accordingly. Ministry with affirmers has been ignored for too long, or forced to conform to rigid constraints of inquirers or new members classes that we have generally known. Frequently the parish pastor has been left alone with the daunting task of identifying, and ministering to, the infinite spiritual needs and questions of all newcomers or returnees to congregational life at once.

This volume's approach to welcoming baptized adults into a congregation's life draws on a variety of precedents, both secular and ecclesiastical. But the book derives content mainly from the writers' experiences of welcoming numerous adults into the life and ministries of many congregations.

Different Parts of the Same Body

Before gathering at the edge of the congregational frontier and embarking on a group trek into the unknown, it is important for us to identify the types of participants in this particular small group ministry. In frontier travel on a wagon train, all participants shared the desire to cross the wilderness, but they did not all share the same motivations or abilities. Similarly, while all participants in this small group ministry must share the common desire for spiritual growth and exploration, each will have different motives and bring different needs and abilities to the travel group. Within this infinite variety of possible backgrounds, three general types of participants might be identified, and each type cultivated and nurtured within a given congregation.

The primary responsibility for developing and shaping this particular ministry with affirmers falls on the guide—a person who might be labeled, in different settings, a facilitator or teacher or convener or coordinator or leader or coach or catechist. Of all these possible titles (and there are, no doubt, other possibilities), the term "guide" best fits the complexity of roles, both obvious and subtle, that will be filled by this individual within this particular small group model.

Who guides a group?

So what are the responsibilities of the guide, and what type of person will make a good guide? A response to the former question is perhaps best contained within the response to the latter. The guide must first be called by God to this ministry. In fact, being called to this role is the only requisite criterion to fulfilling its responsibilities. But what exactly does "being called" mean in this circumstance? The possible answers to this question are many and diverse. Being called to be a guide may be part of a call to the ordained ministry of word and sacrament, but being ordained is certainly not a prerequisite to being a guide. In fact, given the realities of parish life and the demands on a parish pastor's time, most guides will be called from among the laity.

Ordained or not, how does one identify a calling to guide inquirers from the periphery of a congregation into its center? To say this call must come from God is certainly true; but realizing this calling may well require hearing God in the words of others, and seeing God's will in the actions of fellow parishioners. Do

> While the role of guide will be discussed in the singular throughout this chapter, it is certainly possible to fill this role with two or more persons working in close cooperation. In such a team model, however, close attention must be paid to maintaining both trust and continuity on a particular group's journey, with special emphasis accorded to spiritual group building. Perhaps the best method of team leadership in this ministry would be for a given guide to be the primary leader for a given group throughout their journey, with another guide leading the next group, and so on. In this way, guide responsibilities are shared while continuity and trust are maintained within a particular group.

members of the congregation look to a certain individual for guidance in worship, Sunday school, or Bible study? Does a particular member have a history of leadership in spiritual matters or during times of congregational challenge or crisis? Any of these characteristics may be signs of God's calling to be a guide. Additionally, one might turn inward to hear God's call to leadership in this ministry. Is someone at a point in a faith journey where guiding others in a spiritual sojourn might in turn produce spiritual growth within that individual, or where listening to others' needs might in turn help that individual grow in his or her own faith? These inner needs might be an indication of God's call. Or, God's call to this ministry might be very simple and direct—does one desire to welcome outsiders into a congregation, to walk with these inquirers from the edge of the congregational circle into its center, getting to know them along the way? If so, then God's call in this case is obvious.

Beyond this primary call, many other attributes might be helpful in fulfilling the role of guide. A working knowledge of the Bible, worship practices, and the basics of Christian theology and history are necessary during the teaching parts of the journey. Familiarity with congregational resources and congregational history might be useful in planning this ministry and recruiting participants. Certainly a willingness to listen, to care, and to respond with honesty will be important in all parts of this journey.

The first task before the guide is identifying and recruiting the other participants in this journey. There are two other types of participants in this ministry—affirmers and sponsors—and they need to be recruited in equal numbers.

Inquirers

In simplest terms, affirmers (we also use the word *inquirers* interchangeably here) are those outside the congregation who desire to integrate themselves into its life. In the language of parochial tabulation, inquirers are nonmembers or uncatechized persons who wish to participate fully in the church's life. As with most attempts to summarize human needs in administrative shorthand, these terms fail to encompass fully the wide diversity of potential inquirers.

Along with the whole congregation, the guide needs to take an intentional role in seeking out potential inquirers. This will entail greeting unfamiliar persons at worship and congregational functions, and asking if they might be interested in joining the congregation. It might also involve contacting estranged members, asking to visit them, and through a conversation determine if they might wish to become active in the congregation's ministries again. Other inquirers might be reached through announcements in congregational or community media channels, with the guide's name and phone number provided as a contact person. Information and invitations to participate might be offered directly through announcements in worship, Sunday school forums, and selective mailings. In any of these and other possibilities, the

> A call to this ministry, combined with or deriving from both congregational familiarity and congregational leadership, are the essential foundation to becoming a guide. There are also numerous texts for leading small group ministries (see list of resources, p. 111). Finally, regional or national retreats and training sessions, either denominational or ecumenical, in "catechumenate" ministry might be helpful in preparing those who guide.

guide's participation in the day-to-day life of the congregation is essential to identifying and inviting potential inquirers.

Sponsors

The other type of participant in this journey is the sponsor. In simplest terms, a sponsor is a member who is currently active in the congregation's life and who is willing to accompany an outsider on their journey to full participation in the life of the congregation. As with inquirers, sponsors may be—in fact, need to be—of diverse backgrounds. The key aspect of being a sponsor is a willingness to share experiences of the Christian faith. The ministry of sponsors is described in greater detail in the next chapter of this book.

These, then, are the three particular types of participants in this small group ministry—a guide (or guides), inquirers, and sponsors. Beyond these central participants are a large number of indirectly involved persons—an affirmer leadership team, the congregational pastor or pastors, congregational staff (including Christian education directors, church administrators, and church secretaries), congregational leadership (particularly congregation council members and committee chairs), and the entire congregational family. Each of these persons or groups will have the opportunity to support and enhance this small group of travelers as they journey toward the goal of greater participation in the body of Christ.

Forming the Group

Once a list of participants has been established, the task of assembling a particular small group falls upon the guide, in consultation with the pastor and other congregational leaders. First and foremost, inquirers must be paired with sponsors. The number of interested inquirers will determine the number of participant pairs and the number of small groups. While one inquirer-sponsor pair is possible for an inquirers group (which will then consist of three participants, including the guide), a minimum of two or three pairs is preferable, to enhance the opportunities for discussion and sharing. On the other end of the spectrum, five to six pairs may be considered a maximum group size. If more than five or six inquirers desire to join a congregation's life at one time, a second inquirers group (with either the same or a different guide) needs to be formed.

Pairing inquirers with sponsors may be the single most important task for a guide. In many regards, there are no external guidelines for these pairings. The usual criteria for pairing unrelated strangers—criteria such as age, social background, employment, lifestyle, income, family background, or marital status—

> In pairing inquirers and sponsors, one is well-advised to look to pre-existing relationships, but look to them with care and caution. Some pre-existing relationships might be positive sponsor and inquirer pairings, while others could be problematic. In almost all cases, family members, even extended family, would not be considered as sponsors for a given inquirer. The pre-existing family relationship may act to block a free exchange of ideas and experiences. On the other hand, friends, particularly a friend that invited the inquirer to church, might be a good choice for a sponsor, depending on the dynamics of the relationship. Each case must be reviewed individually, with attention paid to any pre-existing relationship that may impede honesty and vulnerability within the particular pair or within the small group. Further, while it is possible for couples to participate in the same group, each person needs to be provided with a separate sponsor appropriate to the individual, not just to the couple.

may actually be impediments to helpful matches. The one criteria that may be relevant here is pairing by gender, a recognition of the probability that, at a certain level, spiritual needs and understandings may differ between men and women.

Personal experience has shown that some of the most meaningful and rewarding pairings of inquirers and sponsors have matched persons who were very different by conventional standards—yet the Spirit nourished these pairs in profoundly enriching ways, and nourished both the group and the congregation through them.

Gathering beside the River of Life

Once the participants in this ministry have been identified and inquirers have been paired (on paper, at least) with sponsors, then a small group of travelers gathers as a group for the first time. How they gather and where they gather will have an impact on the relative success of their journey. Just as west-bound pioneers gathered beside powerful waters of a river before embarking on their journey into the waiting wilderness, so too might a group of inquirers gather with their guide and helpers beside another river—the river of life offered through the waters of baptism.

The font as the point of embarkation for any group of persons preparing to affirm their baptism cannot be emphasized strongly enough. It is at the font that we were made new, and made parts of the same body of Christ. It is a result of our individual baptisms that we gather—both as a small group, and as any group of Christians united in a common task. The font as the origin must be made clear to the group at its start, and revisited often throughout the journey.

As a practical matter, this emphasis might be visually affirmed by holding the first gathering of the group around the church's baptismal font. Further emphasis might be made by asking participants to share memories of their baptism, or of the baptism of someone dear to them. As an ongoing emphasis, group members could be asked to research the date and setting of their baptism. This in turn could be followed by celebrations of baptismal anniversaries as they occur during the group's journey. Constant attention must be paid to reminding the travelers that it is baptism that lies not only at the root of their current involvement in this group and congregation, but also at the center of their life in Christ.

Beyond this baptismal emphasis, at least three other events occur during this first gathering: each participant is given the opportunity to offer information about himself or herself; sponsors are introduced to their inquirers; and the group's future plans are mapped out. The first two subjects might be combined into one by having each sponsor-inquirer pair take fifteen minutes or so (in private, if possible) to conduct reciprocal "interviews." Then upon reassembling the group, each sponsor would introduce her or his inquirer, and each inquirer would introduce her or his sponsor. This format for introductions establishes the concept of shared experience from the outset.

In addition to these essential introductions (of individuals to the group, and of sponsors to inquirers), relevant information about the group's plans is shared by the guide. Distribute a printed handout including contact information provided by participants, along with dates and times for all group meetings and significant events (such as worship times involving the group). It is possible that a group will determine at this first meeting when and where successive meetings are to occur (usually a regular weekly meeting time and place is best), or that time and place might have been predetermined by the guide. Discuss the importance of regular attendance (and a phone call to someone in the group if an absence is unavoidable), the need for confidentiality, and the mutual respect and trust that such confidentiality fosters within the group. Beyond these basic guidelines ("rules of the road," if you will), a bird's eye view of the journey before them might be offered. Two activities—biblical reflection and group prayer—need to be a part of every gathering. If additional topics are planned, provide a sampling of what some of those topics may cover. If a retreat or travel outside the church is anticipated, talk about that. In any case provide sufficient information about the activities of the group to make all involved feel comfortably informed about the journey in front of them. Care must be taken not to restrict the group too greatly. Each group will establish an identity, complete with interests and needs of its own. It is the guide's responsibility to recognize and nurture these needs, changing the group's direction in mid-journey as needed to accommodate this ever-emerging identity.

Once this framework for a group has been shared, a first meeting should be closed with a prayer. Whether this is a group prayer (with each participant contributing a petition or petitions) or a prayer on behalf of the group offered by the guide, the following line from the order for baptism might begin the prayers each time: "By water and the Holy Spirit we are made members of the Church which is the body of Christ."[1] This one sentence summarizes both the starting point and the destination for a small group of affirmers whose journey has now begun.

With the exception of the indicated importance of Bible study/reflection and prayer to the life of the group, the above outline for group activities and duration is intentionally vague, to provide maximum adaptability to specific circumstances and situations. For those interested in more specific suggestions, however, we can also advocate the following:

- The group might meet weekly (less frequently than this will threaten continuity) for ten to fifteen weeks. Longer commitments may be difficult to secure, while shorter duration will reduce the depth and meaning of the experience (keeping in mind that the average small group takes at least three or four meetings just to grow comfortable with one another).
- The group's journey might best symbolically coincide with a journey of the congregation through the church year—for example, the journey may end near one of the baptismal festivals (Easter, Pentecost, All Saints, or the Baptism of Our Lord). In this way, the congregation's life might be reflected in the inquirers group, and the life of the inquirers group might be echoed in the congregation (particularly through the timing of orders of worship involving the group).
- On the matter of discussion topics, one might include the sorts of subjects often shared with newcomers to a congregation or denomination—denominational history and theology, worship practices, the sacraments, and congregational ministries and structure (see appendix B, p. 70). Beyond these obvious possibilities, topics such as social ministry, family needs and issues, living as Christians in a non-Christian world, and the congregation as family might also be considered. Finally, more adventurous activities such as a session spent at a local soup kitchen or homeless shelter—even volunteering to serve on a home-building crew—might be considered, depending on the mix and interest of participants. The key objective, however, is integration of inquirers into the regular life and mission of the congregation. As indicated above, the key is to match the discussion topics and activities

with the needs and interests of the particular group.

Shared Story As Food for the Journey

Writer and teacher Reynolds Price states: "A need to tell and hear stories is essential to the species *Homo sapiens*—second in necessity apparently after nourishment and before love or shelter."[2] For purposes of this discussion, one might be tempted to add the adjective "spiritual" to the noun "stories" in the above quotation. Yet one must guard against defining the parameters of acceptable story too narrowly. A participant's encounter with a stranger at a grocery store or a sudden insight gained at a football game might have as much relevance to that individual's spiritual life and the group's spiritual journey as another participant's reflections on a hymn verse or response to last week's sermon.

An important concept to remember in this context is that one's entire life—young to old, sleeping and waking, work and play, mundane and monumental, sacred and profane—is a spiritual journey. The way in which individuals stitch those infinite moments together into meaningful and cohesive units is through story: stories we tell ourselves in moments of reflection, meditation, prayer, diary entries; and stories we tell each other in conversation, letters, public writings, and group discussion. The inquirers small group will be fed on its journey by its members' stories. A healthy group will be nourished by its shared stories; a struggling group will hunger for shared stories. Ultimately, the participants' stories will combine to become the group's singular story: its identity, its source of sustenance and strength, its repository of shared past (both its past as represented by recollected thoughts and narratives, and its past as represented by the acts of sharing these stories). This story then becomes crucial not only as the group's identity and center, but also as an essential complement of the entire congregation's history and corporate memory. Strengthened and affirmed by the group's own story, the inquirers are able to become a part of the congregation's life and story because they have a story of their own.

Given the importance of shared stories to the group's development and well-being, one must then ask how best to encourage and nurture these stories within the group setting. We must first assert that these stories can grow out of any group topic or activity. The moments of fellowship before or after a group's appointed gathering time foster informal storytelling. A participant might share important information about his or her life in such informal, one-on-one conversation that he or she would be reluctant to volunteer during group discussion. Then, during the group's time, all topics will encourage the sharing of life experiences, though exactly how these experiences are shared may vary depending on the topic and format for discussion. For example, a story—that is, a sharing of life experience by an individual in the group—might also be expressed as a plan for Christian action during a Bible study ("I'm going to take that family a box of clothes"). Sharing of doubts and fears during a discussion on the topic of living as a Christian in a non-Christian world ("I never know what people will think when I do something because Christ tells me to") might later be connected with a petition for guidance and strength offered during a group prayer ("Lord, please show me how to do your will in my life"). While deriving from the same set of experiences and the same complex of needs, each of these shared thoughts and emotions is a glimpse or snapshot of a different aspect of this individual's life, and collectively these glimpses help both this individual and the group better understand God's meaning and purpose for their lives.

God is involved in the sharing of stories—however small or mundane they might seem—because in sharing thoughts and experiences a group begins to trace the power of the Holy Spirit in shaping where they will go as individuals and as the body of Christ.

One might well ask, "These concepts sound good in theory, but how does one get members of a small group to talk about what is important to them?" Given an environment of trust and confidentiality (and not too large a group), people will gladly share important information about their spiritual lives. The key is the setting, which includes both the physical space and the "atmosphere," including the tone of the gathering and the group dynamics. The physical space needs to be informal, but not too informal. A church lounge is a good possibility, or even a small chapel (but only if furniture can be arranged so that participants can face one another). Participants must be comfortable but not disrespectful of one another (no feet on the furniture or lying on the floor).

A typical gathering might start with a chance for each participant to share some key event or thought from the past week. This sharing could be followed by a discussion topic for that day, with topic and content designed to solicit response and discussion from all participants (as opposed to a "lecture"). This discussion in turn could be followed by a lectionary-based Bible study, which might include multiple readings of a passage, followed by multiple reflections and responses (as in the "African" Bible reflection method presented in appendix C, p. 71). Finally, the group could close in prayer, with each member offering a petition and concluding the petition with a repeated phrase (as, "Lord, in your mercy; hear our prayer").

Such a small group format allows for both variety and in-depth reflection. A small group allows for both structure and sufficient flexibility to follow discussion where it leads. Certain themes or ideas may carry through from one activity to the next; so that by the time of prayer, a natural but unconscious unity of thought and response may have permeated the group and be reflected in some of the prayer petitions, and emphasized by the guide in the prayer's introduction or conclusion.

Rites of Passage in Worship

For most inquirers, the only public rite that centers around them is the Affirmation of Baptism. Even this order of worship is frequently minimized or eliminated by congregations. This lack of public occasions that involve the gathered congregation and focus on the inquirers group is unfortunate for two reasons: one, the inquirers group is deprived of direct congregational recognition of its existence, needs, and progress; and two (really the flip side of the first reason), the congregation is deprived of an opportunity to provide direct spiritual support for a ministry that is integral to its growth and sustenance.

If one grants the value for public moments to acknowledge milestones in the life of the inquirers ministry, the next logical question is, how might orders of worship be shaped and conducted for inquirers? Rites designed to prepare persons for affirmation of baptism may include Welcome of Inquirers for Affirmation of Baptism, Calling of the Baptized to Continuing Conversation, and Preparation of Candidates for the Three Days (see appendixes F–H, pp. 81–89). The order of welcome marks the start of the group's journey (and acts as a congregational affirmation and consecration of the ministry). Calling of the Baptized to Continuing Conversion allows the inquirers to declare their desire to join (or become active again in) the congregation. The order of Affirmation of Baptism officially brings affirmers into active (and "confirmed") member status. And the order of Affirmation of the Vocation of the Baptized in the World closes the cycle by allowing new members, sponsors, and the entire membership of the congregation to express their vocations and commitments publicly.

Whatever the number and specific shape of these rites, two important principles need to be kept in mind throughout the life of the affirmers group. First, the affirmers group cannot be allowed to lose sight of the fact that it is part of the congregation, and that its central purpose is to prepare people for active discipleship in the Christian faith. Second, the larger congregation cannot be allowed to forget the affirmers gathered on a spiritual journey within their midst; and that they, the assembled congregation, are called to welcome and nurture these inquirers. Orders of worship focused on the affirmers ministry address both of these concerns, and address them within the context of the congregation's worship life, its most sacred space and time.

The Ocean at the End of the Journey

Bonds will form as the small group of affirmers, sponsors, and guide travel across the wilderness that is the nature of spiritual exploration and growth: between inquirer and sponsor, between all members of the group, and—through orders of worship and congregational prayers—between members of the group and the congregation that surrounds these spiritual travelers. It is these latter bonds—between inquirers and the larger congregation itself—that are the true goal of this particular ministry. These bonds are propagated in many ways—through the sponsor, through the guide, through the pastor, and through congregation members outside the group all working to get to know each inquirer as a unique child of God, with unique needs and gifts.

In this process of recognizing and honoring the individual, it is easier to express the goal than it is to realize it. We must acknowledge that our lives are full, our time is precious, and the six long days between Sundays form a seemingly unbridgeable chasm between knowing someone well enough to nod in passing and really *knowing* that person as a unique child of God. The affirmers group builds just such a bridge through shared time and shared spiritual travel. Further, this bridge is largely built without conscious effort; it accretes over time through shared experiences within the group and between the group and the larger congregation.

Neither the affirmer nor the members of the congregation need to make a special effort to "get to know" one another. That action grows naturally out of shared time and discussion, and grows at a "human" pace, with an affirmer first getting to know an individual (her or his sponsor), then a small group of individuals, and finally the larger group of individuals that comprise the congregational family. The incorporation of inquirer into the congregation is intentionally managed and measured. The rewards to the affirmer as well as to sponsors, guide, and congregation are obvious: a congregational family strengthened in its spiritual interactions, a strengthening that is both its immediate purpose (to serve one another within the family) and its power (providing corporate energy to serve God by serving the world outside the congregation).

How does this ministry end? Or, better phrased, how does the journey of one affirmers group end, so that their ministry within the congregation at large might continue? One might be tempted to dissolve the group immediately following affirmation (or reception into membership). Such a decision would be a mistake, from both a practical and a psychological standpoint. Practically, dissolving the group at this point negates an opportunity to encourage involvement by the new members in the ministries of the congregation. Now that they are members, the former inquirers need the advice and assistance of their sponsors and other small group colleagues to determine how best to involve themselves in specific ministries of the congregation. Representatives of some of the congregation's ministries might be involved at this time to explain the nature and needs of their ministries. Psychologically, it is important to avoid making the new members feel abandoned at this time, the moment they set out to achieve. They need to feel the continued support of the group beyond the order of affirmation itself. Having been brought into membership, they need now to learn how to continue as active members, and they need to learn this with the support and encouragement of their small group.

In short, there is travel yet to be completed beyond the moment of reception into membership. What has to this point been a journey of spiritual discovery and growth focused on incorporating the life of the inquirer into the life of the congregation now becomes a journey of spiritual discovery and growth focused on living one's faith within the life of the congregation. In this sense, this period following reception into membership is analogous with the period following the baptism in the catechumenate. Now especially is a time to focus on Christian vocation, on discerning God's unique call to each of the group's participants (including sponsors and guide, as well as the new members). All the affirmers (that is, each of the participants in the small group) might ask (or be asked): Now that I am a member of this congregation, how has my life changed? And next, what do I do about it?

Group prayer and Bible study continue, though perhaps now with a focus on living one's faith within the congregation. Discussion topics now center around action as much as reflection and information, with specific topics to include such items as stewardship, Christian vocation, and discernment of calling. Care is taken not to make the former inquirers feel pressured into a specific "job" or congregational duty. Rather, some intentional time is spent in observing how existing members live out their faith, and in exploring the possible callings God may have for each of the group's participants.

Aside from building a foundation of action within the congregation, this period provides an opportunity to reflect on the meaning of incorporating these newest members into the congregation. If the moment of reception is the pause (after a long climb) on the high point of land overlooking the sea, then the weeks following are the slow and reflective descent to those blue waters of membership, a descent that can culminate in the affirmation of vocation. These weeks are precious to the group, as they both look back over the path they have traveled together and look forward across the boundless sea that is a life in Christ—in this place and in this Christian community.

Finally, an intentional small group ministry with affirmers calls forth the need for congregations to have various types of small groups available for everyone. Bible study groups, support groups, and service groups need to be an important part of a congregation's ministry. The way to continue the power of a good affirmers group experience is through regular and ongoing participation in the small group ministry of a congregation.[3]

---

1. *Lutheran Book of Worship* (Minneapolis: Augsburg Publishing House, 1978), 121.

2. Reynolds Price, *A Palpable God* (New York: Atheneum, 1978), 3.

3. See *Starting Small Groups—and Keeping Them Going* in the resource list on p. 112.

Chapter 5

Sponsoring Candidates for Affirmation of Baptism

In twenty-first century North America, the word "sponsor" has many different meanings. A sponsor may be a person who invites you to join a private club and vouches for your character, accompanying you through the initiation process. A person in the recovery stage of a twelve-step program may come forward to sponsor another person who is beginning the long and challenging process of recovery. In some parts of the country, "sponsor" holds the same connotation as "godparent" for a child brought for baptism.

Sponsors for adult affirmers are individuals from the Christian community who agree to walk alongside a candidate for affirmation of baptism (also candidates for baptism) in his or her journey to membership in the church. The best sponsor is ultimately active in his or her own spiritual quest and willing to share the details of that journey within the context of a small group. In this sense, the artificial designations of member and nonmember, or active member and inactive member, become secondary, perhaps fading to insignificance as sponsor and affirmer join together in a shared pilgrimage toward spiritual growth and enrichment. There is, then, no hierarchy in this journey, only equals of different backgrounds working toward the same end—a closer relationship with God through greater involvement in one of God's congregational families.

The Sponsor's Role

A sponsor accompanies a candidate for affirmation of baptism throughout the preparation process. The key to a sponsor's role is building a relationship with the affirmer. Through this relationship the larger church community more easily becomes a welcoming place for the affirmer regardless of his or her personal history. The sponsor is a sounding board for the exploration of faith questions or issues that affirmers bring to the process. Sponsors represent the congregation to affirmers by being a primary point of contact and facilitator for integration into the faith community. A sponsor also presents an affirmer to the congregation during the public services of worship that mark the journey, while attesting to an affirmer's readiness to affirm his or her baptism.

The sponsor's role is best described as a companion to the affirmer. A companion walks alongside, neither ahead nor behind, and guides the affirmer along the path of faith formation and spiritual development. Companionship involves both give and take. Sponsors often find that during the faith sharing and storytelling—which are the heart and soul of the journey—affirmers offer questions and insights that provide an engaging and revitalizing faith experience for the sponsor.

Sponsors accompany

Sponsors are also hosts to affirmers, welcoming them to congregational life. A good exercise for sponsors is to walk into the church and intentionally take notice of all the things that are familiar and assume that they are not yet familiar to affirmer candidates. The following ideas are helpful for sponsors to introduce affirmers to church life and community:

- Sit with affirmers at worship and help them become familiar with the liturgy and the unique worship practices in the congregation.
- Introduce affirmers to the availability of worship aids such as hearing devices, large print bulletins and hymnals, and handicapped accessible features, such as an elevator or ramps.
- Take affirmers on a tour of the church facility. Show them the meeting rooms, classrooms, restrooms, and nursery.
- Show affirmers which door to use to enter the church during weekdays or for evening meetings.
- Extend a personal invitation to coffee hour after worship and to other church events.
- Introduce affirmers to other members of the congregation.
- Identify an activity of Christian service that the sponsor and affirmer can do together, such as helping in a soup kitchen or food bank, or visiting homebound members of the congregation together.
- Invite an affirmer candidate to brunch after worship or for dinner in the sponsor's home.

Basically, it is the sponsor who can help the affirmer feel comfortable in a place that may feel unfamiliar. A sponsor can also help the affirmer come to know the people and the practices of the church community.

The traditional method of bringing new members into a congregation may have involved offering a new members class for a certain length of time, anywhere from one to six weeks. Classes were typically led by the pastor, and the newcomers became acquainted with the pastor and other newcomers. After completing the class those who were transferring membership and those affirming their baptism stood in front of the congregation as they were received into membership. While new members may have felt connected to the pastor in some way, this method has not always succeeded in helping newcomers to be connected to the congregation as a whole. Standing before the congregation, the new members might look out into the congregation and see only strangers.

The sponsor's presence serves as a bridge between the congregation and those who are affirming their baptism. The sponsor stands with the affirmer and presents him or her by name to the congregation during public worship and fellowship events. The sponsor lays hands on the affirmer as prayers of blessing are spoken. The sponsor provides a physical connection through use of the voice, the face, the hands, and the touch that connects the affirmer to the whole body of Christ. With sponsors by their sides, affirmers are connected to the congregation in a real and tangible way. Because of the companionship and hospitality extended by sponsors, affirmers are likely to be more fully integrated into the life of the community by the time they affirm their baptism.

Sponsors support

The body of Christ is large and complex, extending far beyond the physical confines of any church building. It is in this community of Christ that Christians come to faith and fullness of life. Support for one another is always important, but it is especially so for those who are being drawn back to life in the church after some time of absence. Sponsors and affirmers should be in regular contact with each other. Sponsors need to check in with affirmers on a regular basis. If an affirmer misses a small group session, the sponsor may call the affirmer or drop by with notes from the session and discuss the topic or scripture passage together. Sponsors may share devotional materials or inspirational reading or tapes with affirmers. Topics for casual conversation might include current events or ethical situations that arise in everyday life (even while acknowledging that there are a variety of issues on which people of faith may differ). Sponsor and affirmer can explore the call of discipleship together and the blessings of living as baptized children of God. The openness of a sponsor to share personal experiences will set the stage for an affirmer to explore the call to ministry in daily life more fully. Most importantly, a sponsor will pray for the affirmer regularly and encourage the affirmer to establish an active life of prayer.

Regular prayer with and for the affirmer is a wonderful opportunity for a sponsor. Daily prayer helps the sponsor focus on the affirmer's spiritual needs. When affirmers know that prayers are made daily on their behalf, they begin to experience the power of the Holy Spirit as they seek to know and trust God. It is also humbling for sponsors to witness the fruit of one's labor as faith grows in the affirmers.

In addition to daily prayer, modeling prayer in small group sessions helps the affirmers learn how to pray. At first, affirmers may only be able to pray with a word or phrase, but as they witness and participate in prayer, they will learn ways to make their requests known to God and to express their joys in thanksgiving.

As affirmers draw near to the time of affirmation of baptism, their experience with prayer may have grown so that they are eager to solicit intercessory prayer on their behalf. A congregational prayer vigil just prior to affirmation of baptism allows congregational members to uphold the affirmers in prayer. The affirmers may even become intercessors for others in the affirmer process. Prayer enriches both the lives of those who pray and those for whom the prayers are offered.

As the relationship grows between the sponsor and the affirmer, it is the sponsor's responsibility to set confidentiality parameters. Small group discussion guidelines prohibit any conversation that takes place within the group from going outside the group. The same is true with the relationship between sponsors and affirmers themselves. As trust develops and lives are shared, an affirmer must feel confident that conversations with a sponsor will not be a topic of discussion during the sponsor's coffee break at work, or at the next weekly Bible study.

A sponsor can be a confidant, but not a therapist. If issues of personal safety, or emotional or psychological well-being surface, the sponsor needs to speak frankly to the affirmer about concern for the affirmer's well being. A sponsor will then encourage the affirmer to speak with the pastor or a professional counselor. If the affirmer is reluctant to do so, the sponsor may offer to make this contact with the affirmer's permission.

Sponsors nurture

Sponsors nurture affirmers by actively listening to questions, observations, insights, and emerging expressions of faith as they are revealed in small groups or casual conversation. As a companion along the journey of faith formation, the sponsor will find that freely sharing the valleys and peaks of one's own life experiences will be as useful in nurturing faith as consulting theological resources to find the "right answer." It is likely that the affirmer will raise questions for which the sponsor has no answer. It is expected that the sponsor will be frank and honest with the affirmer when this happens. Some questions call for a response from faith and experience; others require factual or informational answers. Answers to questions are important, and guides of small groups and clergy play an important role in seeing that scriptural or doctrinal questions are openly received and addressed.

Giving of time and self

The gift of time and self as a sponsor is one of the most precious gifts one can give. Time is always in short supply to meet the requirements of daily living, and it may seem impossible to give any more time to another church commitment. The responsibility of sponsorship cannot be minimized. It requires time and commitment from the sponsor. It is important to remember, however, that as one gives, one also receives.

Time and time again, those who have been sponsors report that the regular rhythm of small group meetings becomes a part of the rhythm of one's life. The disciplines of study, worship, and prayer, along with the relationship that develops with the affirmer, are well worth the investment of time and self. Sponsors frequently report that this intentional time of faith formation spent with an affirmer has been as important for the sponsors themselves as for the affirmer. Church members who are actively engaged in many aspects of congregational life may find that sponsorship provides an opportunity to take a sabbatical from other commitments in order to take time to focus on their own faith formation and spiritual development.

Recruiting Sponsors

By now it is apparent that the role of sponsor is not to be taken lightly. With such responsibility and level of commitment, how are sponsors effectively recruited?

A congregation that is just beginning a more intentional process of working with candidates for affirmation of baptism is best served by prayerful and thoughtful consideration of potential sponsors. Typically, the affirmer leadership team (guides/leaders of small groups, sponsor coordinator, pastors, directors of education, and other congregational leaders) will meet and discuss the people who are known to be exploring a relationship with the church. Personal characteristics, pertinent faith history, and other information that may bear on sponsor selection is shared, always with appropriate discretion. The team spends time in prayer together, mentioning the inquirers and their needs that are known and unknown. Team members seek the guidance of the Holy Spirit in their conversations as they consider potential sponsors.

The methods for identifying sponsors have much in common with the methods for identifying inquirers. The congregational pastor will be an important resource in suggesting possible sponsors. Informational and educational events, such as temple talks, Sunday school forums, or a booth at a ministry fair, can help explain the ministry of sponsorship, and might both diffuse uncertainties (and fears of inadequacy to the task) and inspire interest in this most basic of Christian ministries. Informational articles in congregational media will help raise awareness of the ministry of sponsorship, but these will generally need to be followed by direct contact in the form of a phone call or a visit.

As the ministry of welcoming inquirers is established in a congregation, a list of potential sponsors might be maintained and updated regularly by the new member team, and used to fill sponsorship needs as they arise. As with any emerging ministry, word-of-mouth communication and past-participant suggestions are among the best ways to recruit sponsors. Further, once this ministry is established, former affirmers may desire to become future sponsors. Their experience with the process will make them valued additions to a corps of potential sponsors.

Personal invitations by phone or in person are the most effective recruitment tool for sponsors. General invitations during announcements are effective for introducing the sponsoring concept to the congregation, but rarely result in volunteers. Oftentimes, people feel that they are not qualified to take on the sponsor role. Through individual conversation, the sponsor coordinator can specifically state why the invitation is being extended, and the merits of sponsorship can be explained. Questions and concerns are best addressed by direct response, but printed materials that describe the role of sponsor and the affirmer process are very helpful supplemental tools. After the invitation has been extended, the sponsor coordinator may ask the potential sponsor to consider the request prayerfully for a number of days, after which contact will again be made to receive an answer.

The sponsor coordinator should be a known leader in the congregation who is perceived as trustworthy and genuine. Careful explanation of the affirmer process and information about the particular affirmer that a person is being asked to sponsor helps to personalize the invitation. Drawing connections as to why he or she would make a good sponsor helps persons to identify the gifts he or she will bring to this role. Assurance of sponsor training and ongoing support from the leadership team is critical for people who are considering devoting their time and energy to this ministry.

If a potential sponsor declines, the sponsor coordinator may ask him or her to consider sponsoring at some future time. This allows the conversation to conclude in a respectful and positive manner and opens the door for another invitation later.

Sponsor recruitment may seem to be the most daunting part of the affirmer process, especially when the process is new to a congregation. For some people it is difficult to commit to something that is unfamiliar. Concerns about one's ability to be a sponsor must be addressed patiently and honestly.

When Are Sponsors Recruited?

Ideally, sponsors are connected with candidates in the affirmer process as early as possible. By the time of the first public service when the affirmers are presented to the congregation (see Welcome of Inquirers for Affirmation of Baptism in appendix F, p. 81), sponsors should be by their sides. It is possible to recruit a "stand-in" sponsor in the event that a sponsor cannot be present at one of the public services or for a period of time. The sponsor coordinator or pastor will discuss this situation openly

> Inquirers and sponsors should be made aware of the general nature of the small group ministry they are about to experience, including such information as necessary time commitments, group structure, and an overview of discussion topics. The most important ingredient to the success of this ministry—a willingness both to share and listen—is perhaps hardest to prescribe. While the importance of such openness can be suggested in advance information on this ministry, wise selection of participants, complete with much prayer and an ear to the Holy Spirit, will produce better results in this regard than any informational statements about the importance of spiritual sharing.

with the affirmer so he or she will not feel neglected or abandoned, but cared for and properly supported.

It is possible to recruit a group of sponsors even before the affirmers are all identified. Invitations may be extended to congregational members who seem to be appropriate for sponsorship. They then may stand in the wings, so to speak, until a good match to an affirmer presents itself to the sponsor coordinator or the new member team. At that point, pairing between a sponsor and an affirmer can be made quickly and with confidence.

What Does the Relationship between Sponsors and Affirmers Look Like?

Frequently, a sponsor and an affirmer pair develops an immediate personal friendship, but this is not always the case. A sponsor must not feel that he or she has failed if such a friendship does not develop. Great sponsors are sometimes just casual friends with affirmers. The sponsor coordinator and leadership team need to consider several variables when making matches between sponsors and affirmers. Some affirmers prefer to be matched to people who share similar interests and are at a similar station in life. Others might prefer to be matched with someone who is quite different. Sponsor and affirmer personalities and personal history must be considered when making sponsor selections. Affirmers may be asked whether they have any particular preferences. The leadership team cannot assume that all single people want to be linked with other singles, or overlook a senior member of the congregation when searching for a sponsor for a younger person. If sponsors and affirmers typically attend worship at the same time they will be able to worship together frequently. With rare exceptions, it is a good practice to have same sex matches between sponsors and affirmers, and to refrain from asking a relative or close friend to act as a sponsor. Frequently, affirmers feel freer to express questions or personal faith issues without the dynamics of an established personal relationship that may stand between them and the sponsors.

Supporting the Sponsors

Most congregations engaged in ministry to affirmers will discover the need for a leadership team to direct and care for the process. This team would ideally include at least the following people: pastor, sponsor coordinator, small group coordinator (if there is more than one small group, otherwise just the small group guide/leader), hospitality and communication coordinator, and liturgical ministries coordinator. Particularly in small congregations, one or more of these responsibilities could be assumed by a given individual, but there can be a lot of work for a team to do in a good working new member process. The leadership team takes responsibility for inviting people to the affirmer process, inviting and training sponsors and small group guides, scheduling small group sessions, planning worship services, supporting all the people involved in the affirmer process, and most importantly, holding this ministry before members of the entire congregation.

Throughout the affirmer process, the leadership team needs to provide support for those who have assumed the role of sponsor. Sponsoring is a demanding role, both personally and spiritually. As sponsors accompany, support, and nurture affirmers, they need to be encouraged in their ministry.

Sponsors need to fully understand the affirmer process and their specific role in it. An introductory meeting or training session is a helpful way to explain the process, discuss baptism and affirmation of baptism, and describe the very important role of the sponsor in the process. The training session can be led by the sponsor coordinator or the affirmer team. Members of the leadership team can engage in a sample small group session by playing the role of sponsors, while the prospective sponsors play the parts of affirmers. Roles can then be switched to give sponsors even further experience. The purpose of such role playing is to give the sponsors a feel for what may be expected of them at a regular session. Plenty of time is necessary for questions and answers. Resource materials, such as a sponsor description, small group meeting schedule, and biographical information of affirmers, including address and phone number, should be available. Sponsors need to know who they might contact if further questions arise.

The leadership team should develop a strategy to stay in touch with sponsors. Perhaps regular meetings could be established for sponsors to check in with the team. Sponsors and the leadership team could meet every six to eight weeks for discussion about these topics:

- How is the process going for the sponsor and affirmer?
- Are there particular concerns or unanswered questions that need to be addressed?
- How is the sponsor role fitting?
- How are the small group sessions working?
- What have been the challenges so far?
- What have been the blessings?
- Are there other ways in which the leadership team can help the sponsors in their role?

In short, sponsors can use an opportunity to voice their reactions to the sponsorship role. This discussion also presents an opportunity to make any adjustments that might be necessary and collectively look ahead to the coming weeks.

Another way to enrich the sponsor's experience is to hold a brief prayer service for sponsors. An excellent time for this might be just before the beginning of Lent or at other times just a few weeks before affirmation of baptism is scheduled to occur. The pastor may extend an invitation to sponsors and other congregational members for a time of quiet meditation. The scriptures may be read and then, one by one, perhaps with the laying on of hands, each sponsor should be named in prayer. Individual prayers may include petitions for the sponsor's continuing faith journey, personal needs and requests, as well as guidance for his or her role as a sponsor.

The supportive power of prayer throughout the affirmer process is upheld before all participants, including the entire congregation. As the worshiping community regularly names affirmers during the prayers of the church, so are sponsors named in prayer. The work of sponsorship can be exhilarating, exhausting, uplifting, and challenging. Both affirmers and sponsors need the support of the entire congregation as they journey together.

Sponsorship and Congregational Renewal

One of the benefits of ministry with affirmers is congregational renewal. A number of members become involved in this ministry as leadership team members, guides, and sponsors. Through the journey, they often experience a renewal of their own faith. For sponsors, the opportunity to be engaged in the faith development of individuals seeking growth in Christ makes the mission of the church acutely clear. Church membership is about more than helping to pay a congregation's mortgage or recruiting for various positions of leadership. It is most essentially about the witness of Christ in the world. The great commission in Matthew 28 calls all Christians to "make disciples of all nations." This is the mission of the church. After a congregation has engaged in a deepened ministry with affirmers for a sustained time, a renewed sense of mission begins to emerge. Council members who have been sponsors or affirmers carry this sense of mission and discipleship into council deliberations and their vision for the ministry of the congregation.

By the time the celebration of Affirmation of the Vocation of the Baptized in the World (see appendix J, p. 99) has taken place, the entire congregation has prayed for, supported, and nurtured sponsors and affirmers for many months. In worship services, and the weekly prayers of the church, through newsletter articles and bulletin announcements, participants in the new member process have been named. Something special is obviously happening. A profession of faith made by adults who have diligently prepared to affirm their baptism publicly is a moving event to the congregation. As witnesses to this growth in faith, the congregation's members are renewed in their own confession and commitment. As the affirmer process transforms a congregation, so the mission of the church is transformed.

The gift of this ministry to the church is that it gathers the faith community around the invitation to know Christ. Life with Christ begins at the baptismal font and ends when we join the community of saints who have lived and died in Christ. In between, we walk, run, stand still, and sometimes lose our way along the journey of faith. Along the way there are others who travel with us. They accompany, encourage, challenge, listen, and pray. They show us the way when we are lost, and they never let go. They are the community of saints. They are also sponsors. They personally claim their call to discipleship and prayerfully accompany others who are coming *home* to the refreshing and life-giving waters of baptism and to the community that claims them in Christ.

Ten Activities for Sponsors and Affirmers

- Pray for your affirmer each day.
- Invite your affirmer to coffee hour or an adult education class.
- If your affirmer has children, offer to sit with them one Sunday.
- Invite your affirmer to attend a parish activity with you.
- Give your affirmer a call on a rainy day just to say you are thinking of him or her.
- Check-in by phone with your affirmer when a small group meeting is missed.
- Tell your affirmer a story about when you joined the congregation.
- Volunteer at a local food bank or homeless shelter with your affirmer.
- Introduce your affirmer to at least three members of the congregation each week.
- Pray for your affirmer every day.

Chapter 6

Experience As a Teacher of Theology

A few decades ago, a social psychologist invited a group of children to play a board game with some adults. In the course of the game, all of the participants won some money that they were allowed to keep. At the end of the game, the experimenter talked about a charity to which the players might want to donate some of their winnings. The adults, who were cooperating with the experimenter, were then required to do one of four things:

- They were to speak about the importance of giving money to charities and then donate some of their winnings.
- They were to speak about the importance of charitable donations, but then, contrary to their words, keep everything they had won.
- They were to express no opinion and donate no money.
- They were to give money to the charity but not express any opinion about the merits of such action.

In the situations where the adults' words and actions were consistent, the children's behavior mimicked the behavior of the adults, that is, the children held on to their money or gave their money to charity, respectively. In the situation where the adults spoke about the importance of giving money, and actually gave their money to charity, the children likewise gave their money to charity. Similarly, when the adults spoke about the importance of giving money to charity, but kept their money, the children also kept their money. The study concluded that, regardless of what was *said* by the adults, the children patterned themselves after what the adults *did*. The adult words did not seem to have an impact on the children's choice of actions; the adult behavior made all the difference.[1]

Learning Theology in the Early Church

Much like the process of learning in the game above, *catechesis*, or instruction in the Christian faith, is a process whereby individuals learn to pattern their behavior after the behavior of others whom they respect. Quite a variety of people have spoken in recent years about the importance of a patterning approach to adult faith formation. A person's commitment to stewardship, lifelong learning, care for others in community, service to the neighborhood, and even hospitality to strangers is at its most basic level a response learned through experience in the Christian community.

Learning faith through experience has long been the primary method of instruction in cultures where literacy rates were seldom higher than two or three percent of the population.

Early Christians often described their journey of faith in terms of demands, celebrations, duties, and rewards experienced within the larger community. The author of Acts observes:

> Now the whole group of those who believed were of one heart and soul, and no one claimed private ownership of any possessions, but everything they owned was held in common. The apostles gave their testimony to the resurrection of the Lord Jesus, and great grace was upon them all. There was not a needy person among them, for as many as owned lands or houses sold them and brought the proceeds of what was sold. They laid it at the apostles' feet, and it was distributed to each as any had need. Day by day, they spent much time at home and ate their food with glad and generous hearts, praising God and having the goodwill of all the people. And day by day the Lord added to their number those who were being saved (Acts 2:42–47; translation prepared by the author).

While the book of Acts was not intended to be read as history, this small snapshot of life in the early church correlates three important values that it had, namely: community wisdom (the people had one heart and soul), community service (those who owned land or houses sold them and brought the proceeds of what was sold to be shared among the others) and community outreach (day by day the Lord added to their number those who were being saved).

In our modern age of general literacy, it is not always self-evident that for early followers the Christian experience was first and foremost just that—an experience. In the case of the Acts text above, the Christian experience was one of shared abundance in the midst of a world that ordinarily did not have this practice. In a recent study called *The Rise of Christianity*, sociologist Rodney Stark argues that the rapid growth in Christianity over the first few centuries was due in great part to the influence of friends and the material care that Christians provided for one another.[2] Indeed, the very name for church in Greek, *ekklesia*, means "those called together," because in the early Christian world-view there was no learning about God that was not somehow also a patterned response to community life.

Learning Theology Today

If Christian teaching and practice from its earliest traditions has been shaped by community experience, then it makes sense to ask what community-based, experiential learning looks like in our own age. As early as the 1970s religious educators were talking about the need for Christian education, especially among adults, to be both experiential and flexible. Classrooms are not the most significant locus of adult learning, nor is simply passing along information the basic purpose of religious education. Rather, the goal of religious education is to engage in communal theological reflection so that human experience can be given *value*. In the language of educators, the purpose of adult learning is to "embody the Word."[3]

As the church continues to make room for the needs of adult learners and the unique needs of adult inquirers, we begin to see that catechetical theology is more properly a *methodology*. This methodology offers a dynamic process of theological reflection on patterned behavior whose content is the infinite variety of human experience.

While there certainly are times when it is important to convey doctrine, it is simply not the end goal of Christian catechesis. The catechetical process is a time in which the Christian community gives worth to the entirety of human experience. Only as we learn to evaluate and place worth on our own and each other's experience of the world can we then allow ourselves to empathize with the struggle of a neighbor, be confronted by a text of scripture, attend to the movement of the Spirit, or otherwise engage in theological reflection.

Trusting Life Experience

In order to place value on our own or others' experiences, we need to affirm that reflection on human experience can be used as a vehicle for the revelation of God. Many who have learned the phrase *sola scriptura* may find it difficult to acknowledge forms of revelation apart from the scriptures. Yet, in *The Freedom of a Christian* Martin Luther argues that righteousness and freedom can be neither sullied by insincere religious affectation on the one hand, nor harmed by ordinary life experience on the other.

> It does not help the soul if the body is adorned with the sacred robes of priests or dwells in sacred places or is occupied with sacred duties or prays, fasts, abstains from certain kinds of food, or does any work that can be done by the body and in the body. The righteousness and the freedom of the soul require something far different since the things which have been mentioned could be done by any wicked person. Such works produce nothing but hypocrites. On the other hand, it will not harm the soul if the body is clothed in secular dress, dwells in unconsecrated places, eats and drinks as others do, does not pray aloud, and neglects to do all the above-mentioned things which hypocrites can do.[4]

If Christians are to become fully involved with the variety and wonder of ordinary life, two things are important to remember. First, scripture can have a unique power to speak when it takes its place as part of God's dialogue with humanity. When scripture is treated first and foremost as a story of God's people, then a person's own life story and the narrative of his or her community instantly become part of a larger history. This understanding of scripture helps people begin to value life and see discrete occurrences as woven into a larger historical tapestry. Scripture then has the power to affirm and critique our unique life experiences and give them worth. In the context of a truth-telling community that regularly reflects on the larger story of God's people, personal storytelling even has the power to transform lives.

Second, we also affirm incarnational theology when we value experience as a teacher. We are not only made in the image of God, but through baptism we are also a priesthood of believers: we are God's hands and feet. Part of the work of catechesis is to expect divine revelation in every person we meet. No one is outside of God's work in the world. Catechetical theology is always a servant of life experience because it trusts that God is powerfully revealed in ordinary life.

The Only One without Gloves On

Many people active in the hospice movement have discovered that ministry is not preaching or even primarily speaking at all, but simply holding people's hands and sharing communion with them. These two things proclaim the simple theological message *you are accepted* to people who otherwise are kept at arms length by society. Holding hands and sharing communion may be a hospice minister's primary job. A hospice staff person recently noted, "I am often the only person on the floor without gloves on." Her simple acts of holding hands and sharing communion are the fullest possible expressions of her theological understandings.

This woman was not always convinced that theology must grow out of practice. When she first began her chaplaincy she discovered that it was often easy to speak memorized God-talk, especially when faced with a difficult situation or an awkward silence. As she grew more comfortable with her work, however, and as she questioned her own role as someone who embodied God for others, she came to realize that her words were primarily focused on her and did not necessarily reflect the experiences of the people she sought to serve. Over time, this caring woman let her experience on the hospice floor inform her theology and shape it until her theology became integrated with the realities of life in the hospice ward.

Doing Church with Luther

In ministry with the adult inquirer, theology is always in conversation with daily life. Dare we say the days are over when we would echo Luther's phrase that others should attend to their catechetical studies in order to "repeat what they have heard and give a correct answer when they are questioned."[5]

We live in a world of communication overload. Machines in almost any office these days give witness to this fact: we are surrounded by telephones with connections to voice mail, fax machines, and computers with connections to the Internet and high-speed printers. Many church office workers spend as much time trashing unread e-mail and dodging unsolicited faxes each morning as they ever do reading scripture or reflecting on their own existence. Discerning what is of value and integrating what is fundamentally important can be difficult in such a world.

Yet as we spend time in reflection with other people of faith, as we read the larger story of God's people through the scriptures, and regularly listen to other people's experience of life in order to discover what is of worth for them, we become more practiced in doing the same for ourselves. Perhaps this is Luther's intention in the Large Catechism despite the previous quote. He also says, "Thus [we] shall be led into the Scriptures, and make constant progress in same. It is not enough to learn only the words and be able to repeat them."[6]

One of the gifts Luther gave the church was his knowledge that ongoing learning is at the heart of Christian faith and life.

> We must enlighten those who are to come after us and fill our offices and do our work, that they in turn may bring up their children to be fruitful in good deeds. Thus God's Word and Christianity shall be upheld. Therefore, let every head of a family remember that he is under obligation, by virtue of the injunction and command of God, to teach or have taught to his children the things they ought to know. Since they are baptized and received into the Christian communion, they ought likewise to enjoy this fellowship of the Lord's Supper that they may serve us and be useful. For we need the help of them all in our attempt to believe, to love, to pray and to fight the devil.[7]

Someone has said recently that the first thousand years of the church belonged to the bishops, the second thousand years to the priests, and the third millennium belongs to the laity. Perhaps we are finally getting the hang of things five hundred years after Luther expressed his vision of a priesthood of all believers. If the third millennium of the church belongs to ordinary Christians who allow life to bear witness to the mystery of God, then we are now on the threshold of an exciting time.

Conclusion

The social psychologist who studied children's responses to adult charity told us what we, in many ways, already knew: people learn from the actions of others. The early church instinctively knew the importance of theology that grew out of life in the community of believers. When in our own day instruction in the Christian faith places value on experience, then faith becomes an integral part of life. To this end, catechetical theology is a methodology: it is a process of theological reflection that trusts human experience even as it engages in dialogue with scripture and community life. When we enter the process of working among inquirers with the assumption that human experience is the best teacher of theology, we help to increase others' faith and help build up the church. Ultimately, ministry with the adult inquirer has everything to do with learning how to learn from life in the hope that, through reflection on life, the people of God will also grow to be good citizens of earth.

---

1. This study was cited in a lecture on social psychology at the University of Waterloo in 1981.
2. See Rodney Stark, *The Rise of Christianity: A Sociologist Reconsiders History* (Princeton: Princeton University Press, 1996). Chapter 1, in particular, outlines the dramatic rise in Christian affiliation due primarily to friendship groupings and the distribution of shared wealth. For an account of Christian beginnings from an historical and archeological perspective see John Crossan, *The Birth of Christianity* (New York: HarperSanFrancisco, 1998), chapters 12 and 13.
3. John H. Westerhoff, III, *Inner Growth Outer Change: An Educational Guide to Church Renewal* (New York: The Seabury Press, 1979), 55–62.
4. *Martin Luther's Basic Theological Writings*, ed.Timothy Lull (Fortress Press, 1989), 597.
5. Martin Luther, *Luther's Large Catechism*, trans. J.N. Lenker (Minneapolis: Augsburg Publishing House, 1967), 9.
6. Ibid.
7. Ibid, 153

Chapter 7

Ministry in Daily Life

St. Augustine's words are surprising, even startling: *Be what you see, and receive what you are.* How is it possible for us to be what we can see? How can we receive what we already are? Living in the fifth century, St. Augustine, bishop of Hippo in North Africa, spoke these words as part of a sermon preached on the Day of Pentecost. He was speaking to those who had been baptized just fifty days before at the Vigil of Easter, and he was referring to the bread and wine on the altar before him.

He began by explaining the purpose of his sermon: "What you see on the Altar of God, you saw on the [Easter] night that has passed. But what it is, what it means, how it contains the sacrament of something great, that you have not yet heard." He continued: "If therefore you are the body of Christ and his members, your mystery has been put on the Lord's table. You receive your mystery. You respond 'Amen' to what you are, and by responding you sign your name to it." Then he concluded: "Be what you see, and receive what you are."[1]

The words are startling. They jump out like unmatched plaids or garish colors set side by side. Perhaps it is a riddle, but very likely not. These words are a call to ministry—the ministry in daily life of all the baptized. They have implications, not only for our life in Christ, but for our worship and liturgy, our theology and spirituality, and our calling to matters of peace and justice. These words can serve as the introduction to a discussion of ministry in daily life following the sacrament of baptism. The place to begin is with baptism itself.

Holy Baptism

By the water and word of baptism, we are joined both to the death and to the resurrection of Jesus Christ. Baptism is both death and birth simultaneously. This dialectical tension is mirrored clearly in the scriptures:

> Do you not know that all of us who have been baptized into Christ Jesus were baptized into his death? Therefore we have been buried with him by baptism into death, so that, just as Christ was raised from death by the glory of the Father, so we too might walk in newness of life (Romans 6:3-4).
>
> Nicodemus said to [Jesus,] "How can anyone be born after having grown old? Can one enter a second time into the mother's womb and be born?" Jesus answered, "Very truly, I tell you, no one can enter the kingdom of God without being born of *water* and *Spirit*" (John 3:4-5).

All who are baptized have been joined to the death and resurrection of Jesus Christ—

regardless of age. What is true for all in the sacrament of baptism is also a significant part of the preparation for baptism of those who are of an age to be prepared.

In the catechumenate—as described in *Welcome to Christ* (see resources section at the end of this book)—unbaptized adults journey through a time of inquiry, catechumenate, and baptismal preparation prior to administration of both sacraments (baptism and communion). This journey is accompanied by baptized members of the congregation—sponsors, catechists, pastors, and others. This journey is also marked by both death and life. Baptism is not only death of an old self, it is also the death of an old life. Adults who come seeking baptism are leaving an old life behind—just as much as they are taking on a new life. Baptism is not only the birth of a new person, but also the beginning of a new life in Christ. All of this is the work of the Holy Spirit. As Martin Luther writes in his explanation to the third article of the Apostles' Creed:

> I believe that by my own understanding or strength I cannot believe in Jesus Christ my Lord or come to him, but instead the Holy Spirit has called me through the gospel, enlightened me with his gifts, made me holy, and kept me in the true faith.[2]

It is this "calling, gathering, enlightening, and making holy" work of the Holy Spirit that is active in the preparation of adults for baptism. Those who are new to the faith and who come seeking guidance or companionship on their journey are nurtured and fed in the womb of the church over time. For some this may be a relatively short period of time, and for others a longer time. Regardless of the duration, there is one common theme—those preparing for baptism are journeying toward a sacrament which is both their death and their birth.

Affirmation of Baptism

Herein lies a thread also woven into the order of Affirmation of Baptism. Those who come to Christ's church for an affirmation of baptismal faith—perhaps even a faith that has not been nurtured or fed within the church for many years—are being "called, gathered, enlightened, and made holy" by the Holy Spirit. Affirmers are also are on a journey that involves both death and new life.

At the same time, it must be stated clearly: affirmers are not catechumens—persons preparing for baptism. Our baptismal theology prevents us from pretending that affirmers—even those with no formal association with Christ's church since the day of baptism—are not already part of Christ's church. Faith may be only that of an infant. Yet all the baptized are children of God—heirs by birth, if not by active participation in the community of faith. We dare not treat any of the baptized as if they are not already God's daughters and sons.

This means the journey of an affirmer is both unlike and like that of a catechumen. Affirmers are already joined to Jesus Christ in baptism. An adoption has taken place. Gifts of the Holy Spirit in baptism have already been offered. At the same time, there is much calling, gathering, enlightening, and making holy yet to be done. There is a journey involving both life and death that remains. Just as baptism is not only the death of an old self, but also of an old life, so an affirmation of faith—especially when there has been no previous life of active Christian faith—involves leaving an old life behind and taking on a new one. An affirmation of baptismal faith is the death of an old way of life, as well as the nurture and growth of a new one. The Holy Spirit is enkindling new life and new faith. For adult affirmers—those baptized as infants or children, but with years of inactivity—what remains is a journey: a journey of faith, a journey of life and death.

Vocation

All of this points to an understanding of Christian vocation advanced by Martin Luther, who defined vocation far more broadly than any one particular occupation or relationship that is ours. Christian vocation is not defined by a specific occupation or relationship at all. Rather, our vocation is our baptismal calling to life in Christ. This vocation is given life and breath in every setting—every job, every relationship, every opportunity and activity—in which faith is lived out. Vocation is lived out in the many roles—or *offices*, as Luther called them—that are ours: carpenter or physician, daughter or son, neighbor or coworker, Sunday school teacher or choir member. It is in the many choices and decisions we make each and every day in these offices that we either honor or dishonor Christ and the Christian calling that is ours in baptism. Christian vocation always points to Christ, both as its source and as its focus.

Our vocation is lived out by everything we are and do in order to live out two things: love of God and service to our neighbor. This vocation—another name is *ministry*—of the baptized, regardless of age, position, or title, is the same: to love God, and to serve our neighbor. The specifics and particulars may be, in fact, will be, different for each and every Christian. But the calling is the same. We are called by God in Christ, through the work of the Holy Spirit, to love God and to serve our neighbor. This is our vocation; this is our call to ministry in daily life. Thus, it is not only appropriate, but essential that both those preparing for baptism and those preparing to affirm their baptismal faith wrestle with the same questions: To what are we called by our baptism? How will that calling be lived out in daily ministry? Ministry in daily life is both a gift and a charge—to the baptized, and the soon-to-be baptized alike—to die daily and be born in Christ.

Practices of the Faith

Throughout the process of faith formation—for unbaptized persons and affirmers alike—it is the basic and fundamental practices or disciplines of the Christian life that are taught and practiced—namely: worship, prayer, scripture reading, and ministry in daily life. These practices make an apprenticeship in the faith. It is an apprenticeship we never leave. Just as an apprentice of some kind of trade must learn the use of basic tools in order to grow—for a carpenter, for example, they are hammer, saw, level, and square—so those who are new to life in Christ learn the tools of worship, prayer, scripture reading, and ministry in daily life in order to grow continually in the life of faith. In order for life to grow out of the death and birth of baptism, the disciplines of the Christian life are essential.

Any discussion of ministry in daily life must take place in this context. Ministry is one of the disciplines of the faith. It is not the only one. Worship, prayer, and the regular reading and study of scripture are other disciplines. Together these four form the foundation of the disciplined Christian life. Together they help to shape our response to the vocational calling that is ours in baptism.

A Definition

In a word, ministry in daily life is *living*—the day to day living out of our baptismal calling to love God and serve our neighbor. It is the ongoing fluid-like stream of choices, activities, and events—both great and small—that form the ebb and flow of daily life. And throughout them all, God in Christ, by the activity of the Holy Spirit, continues to feed and nourish, guard and guide us in our living.

One of the great mysteries of the faith is this: we can neither clearly identify nor fully recognize all the ways in which our God showers the gifts of grace upon us. We are never fully aware of the measure of gifts by which God strengthens us for the living out of ministry in daily life. Yet this mystery is not completely unknowable. Some things we know with the certainty of faith, for we have the gracious promise that God in Jesus Christ comes to us through very concrete and tangible means, namely the word and sacraments. So the question is this: What is the place of word and sacrament for ministry in daily life?

The Word of God

The word of God calls us out of death to new life. As St. Paul wrote in Romans, quoting Hosea:

> "Those who were not my people
> I will call 'my people,'
> and her who was not beloved
> I will call 'beloved.'
> And in the very place where
> it was said to them,
> 'You are not my people,'
> there they shall be called
> children of the living God"
> (Romans 9:25-26).

The word both calls us out of an old life and points us toward a new life in Jesus Christ. It is a twofold action: leaving an old life behind and putting on new life in Christ. Paul stated this clearly: "So if anyone is in Christ, there is a new creation: everything old has passed away; see, everything has become new!" (2 Corinthians 5:17).

The word calls us. Each and every time the scriptures are read, preached, or taught, Christ the living Word calls us once again. It happens at first hearing. Those preparing for baptism and those preparing for affirmation of baptism receive the same call.

This is a calling both to forgiveness and to repentance. By the life, death, and resurrection of Christ, the cosmic battle between God and the Evil One has been won—death has ultimately been conquered. It is this crucified, risen, and victorious Christ who comes to us in our hearing of the word of God. By this word God offers forgiveness of sins and repentance—a turning of our face toward God and toward a disciplined life in Christ. We are called to a regular practice of our faith by the disciplines of worship, prayer, scripture, and ministry in daily life. This calling of the word acts simultaneously to strengthen and to challenge us. We are strengthened by the gracious promise of forgiveness, acceptance, and love in Jesus Christ. At the same time, we are continually called to new living that is our ministry in daily life. Both theological statements are true:

- We are reconciled to God in Jesus Christ.
- We are called to newness of life each day.

This tension is at the heart and center of ministry in daily life. For while this ministry is not the prerequisite to new life in Christ, it is the expectation for our daily living and dying in Christ. The word of God calls us. The word strengthens us. The word also challenges us.

The Lord's Supper

One of the church's eucharistic prayers includes these words:

> Send now, we pray, your Holy Spirit, the spirit of our Lord and of his resurrection, that we who receive the Lord's body and blood may live to the praise of your glory and receive our inheritance with all your saints in light.[3]

Here once again is the twofold movement. By invoking the Holy Spirit, in order that we "may live to the praise of your glory" and also "receive our inheritance with all your saints in light," we are called both to death and to rebirth.

We are called to death and new life by our participation in the life, death, and resurrection of Jesus Christ. In eating the body and drinking the blood of Christ we are joined to

Christ's own death and resurrection. We die with Christ at each eating and drinking of the Lord's supper, and we are raised with him to new life in the kingdom of God. At each celebration of the Lord's supper, we are again fed and nourished for new life in Christ.

Ministry in daily life is a reflection of this sacramental dying and rising. Each and every time we receive the body and blood of Jesus Christ we are graciously nourished and turned toward ministry. It is as if we cannot eat the bread of Christ without also having our faces turned toward those who are without bread. Their hunger becomes our hunger. Likewise, we cannot drink wine without seeing those who are thirsty, or hurting, or homeless, or abused, or lonely, or dying. Ministry in daily life springs from the eating and drinking of bread and wine because it is Christ's body and blood that we eat and drink. Joined to Christ, all who are our neighbors become those for whom we continually die and are raised to new life.

The Lord's supper—like the scriptures—is the lifeblood of ministry in daily life. It brings life to us—both the new life of Christ's resurrection, and our own newness of life through Christ's gracious forgiveness and love. The Lord's supper also impels us toward Christ's ministry to all who are in need. It is as if there has been a great exchange—Christ's life for ours, and our old way of living for new life in God's kingdom.

The Joyful Exchange

Martin Luther wrote of this very mystery in his treatise "The Blessed Sacrament of the Holy and True Body of Christ, and the Brotherhoods" in *Word and Sacrament I* from 1519. He wrote first of the bread and wine themselves:

> For just as the bread is made out of many grains ground and mixed together, and out of the bodies of many grains there comes the body of one bread, in which each grain loses its form and body and takes upon itself the common body of the bread; and just as the drops of wine, in losing their own form, become the body of one common wine and drink—so it is and should be with us, if we use this sacrament properly.

This, in turn, becomes *Christ's* exchange:

> Christ with all saints, by his love, takes upon himself our form (Phil 2:7), fights with us against sin, death, and all evil.

Which, in turn, becomes our *own* exchange:

> This enkindles in us such love that we take on his form, rely upon his righteousness, life, and blessedness. And through the interchange of his blessings and our misfortunes, we become one loaf, one bread, one body, one drink, and have all things in common.

Truly, it is a sacramental mystery:

> O this is a great sacrament, says St. Paul, that Christ and the church are one flesh and bone. Again through this same love, we are to be changed and to make the infirmities of all other Christians our own; we are to take upon ourselves their form and their necessity, and all the good that is within our power we are to make theirs, that they may profit from it. That is real fellowship, and that is the true significance of this sacrament. In this way we are changed into one another and are made into a community by love. Without love there can be no such change.[4]

All of this is brought into sharp relief in the context of weekly worship.

Christian Worship

As the community of Christ's body gathers each week for worship, the word of God is proclaimed and the sacraments are celebrated. By gathering, the community of faith and its individual members are renewed and strengthened in faith and life. While word and sacrament are at the heart and center, the shape of worship is sometimes overlooked as a source of renewal and strength. In our daily dying and rising, the liturgy of the church is central.

This centrality is certainly true of the broad sweep of Christian liturgy—from gathering to sending. At the same time, individual portions of the church's liturgy carry particular significance. Without being exhaustive, we can name the following as sources of both strength for and challenge to our individual ministry in daily life.

Confession and Forgiveness

We confess our bondage to sin and our failure to love God with our whole heart or our neighbor as ourselves. In turn we receive God's forgiving power in Jesus Christ in the declaration of forgiveness. In all of this we experience, once again, a baptismal death and new birth. More than addressing specific or particular sins alone, confession and forgiveness speaks also to the daily dying and rising of our whole self in Christ. We become a new creation. The Order for Confession and Forgiveness is a gift of the Holy Spirit's power for renewed ministry in daily life.

Creed

As the gathered Christian community confesses the creed in worship, individually we also renew the faith and promises of our baptism. The Apostles' Creed in particular is a verbal and faith-filled call to baptismal renewal. In the creed we confess not only the dying and rising of Jesus Christ, but also our own. We once again pass over from death to new life and receive the gracious gifts of God in Christ for our ministry in daily life.

Prayers of the Church

In the petitions of the prayers we pray for Christ's church, the world, and all of God's creation. We pray also for specific individuals—both those we know personally, and those we may not know—whose needs become known to us. As the petitions are read and prayed, our eyes open to the needs of our neighbors. In our baptismal calling to love God and to serve our neighbors, we struggle daily with the needs of others that can be met by our own individual gifts and resources and those of the Christian community. The weekly opening of our eyes in the prayers of the church is an exercise in discernment. We discern our ability to meet the needs of those for whom we pray. In the process we discover our own ministry in daily life.

Peace

As the peace of the Lord is shared in worship, we make peace with one another before bringing our gifts to the altar. This is not by accident. In the Sermon on the Mount, Jesus instructed the crowd gathered before him: "So when you are offering your gift at the altar, if you remember that your brother or sister has something against you, leave your gift there before the altar and go; first be reconciled to your brother or sister, and then come and offer your gift" (Matthew 5:23-24). The peace is both a call to, and an experience of, reconciliation in Christ. In the experience of receiving forgiveness, we share in the dying and rising of Jesus Christ. To ask forgiveness of another is to die to our own sin. To offer forgiveness is to participate in Christ's gracious and life-giving work. As we practice this ministry we are renewed both in faith and in life.

Offering

In the passing of collection plates filled with identical paper envelopes, it is sometimes difficult to remember that the offering is so much more. Just as the early church accepted not only money, but also clothing and food—including bread and wine for the eucharist—

we are called to offer more of ourselves. Our eyes are opened to the needs of our neighbors when we come to understand that offering is more than the giving of things. It is the giving of our very selves to those who are in need. In the context of Christian worship, the offering is a death and a rebirth. Not only do we die to our dependence on and accumulation of things for our self identity, but we also are raised to a new identity—one formed in the waters of baptism, fed by the bread and wine of the Lord's supper, and nourished by the word and the community of believers. Our calling to love God and to serve our neighbors is both defined and tested by the offering in worship.

Dismissal

As the gathered Christian community is sent into the world for mission and ministry, the dismissal begins with the words: "Go in peace." The congregation has already shared the peace. Now it is sent out in that same peace. It is the peace of Christ that sustains us. It is also the peace of Christ that marks and forms us for ministry. Still, there is one additional word of admonition: "Serve the Lord." This returns us, for one final moment, to the waters of baptism. As we understand our baptismal calling or vocation to include two parts—to love God and to serve our neighbor—so we are sent out with that calling ringing in our ears. We are called to ministry in daily life, a ministry that includes our daily death and rebirth. We respond: "Thanks be to God."

Stewardship

The biblical teachings of Jesus give witness to a complex and variegated understanding of Christian stewardship.[5] Among the requirements of a good steward is faithfulness to the will and desire of the master. This is clear in the words of Jesus that conclude the parable of the dishonest manager: "Whoever is faithful in a very little is faithful also in much; and whoever is dishonest in a very little is dishonest also in much" (Luke 16:10). To be a Christian steward is to be faithful to God. Faithfulness is both the guiding word from our baptismal calling and the direction for our ministry in daily life.

To be faithful to the will and desire of God in Jesus Christ involves both a death and a rising to new life on our part. Faithfulness to God's calling and command does not come naturally for us. It is not part of our human nature. This has to do with sin—that inclination and inbred orientation within us that both causes and allows us to turn our face away from God continually. We are selfish by our very nature. Left to our own devices, we care more for ourselves than for anyone or anything else. We are faithful to ourselves more than we are to God. To act otherwise requires that our selfish nature first be put to death.

As we return each day to our baptism, this selfish nature is drowned in the baptismal waters once again. By our regular participation in the Lord's supper, a new person is reborn—one who is faithful, not only to God, but also to our calling to Christian stewardship. By returning daily to our death in baptism, we are renewed and strengthened each day for a life of stewardship—being faithful to the will and desire of God in Jesus Christ.

All that we are, and all that we own belongs to God. This we know, not only because God is the creator of all that is, but also because God is the redeemer and sustainer of all. Everything belongs to God—even our very selves. Christian stewardship begins when we recognize that this is true. More than that, it involves living as though this is true. Stewardship involves action. It is at this point that the disciplines of the faith come into play.

The disciplines of worship, prayer, the

reading of scripture, and ministry in daily life are part of our Christian stewardship. By engaging in these disciplines regularly we are being faithful to God. More than that though, we are returning to our baptismal death and rebirth. By the power of the word and sacraments we are once again joined to Christ's death and resurrection. We are offered forgiveness of sins and we are called to repentance. We are strengthened in the daily decisions and activities of life and we are challenged to grow in faith. By our own practice of these basic and fundamental disciplines of the faith, we die to our own sinfulness and are raised to a life of renewed faithfulness in Christ.

Stewardship is more than the giving of money—much more. To limit Christian stewardship to the giving of money—or perhaps even to the giving of time or possessions—is to forget and ignore the power of our death and rebirth in Jesus Christ. At the heart and center of our stewardship is this death and birth. Out of this springs our practice of faithfulness to God, who has entrusted to us gifts belonging not to us but to God.

Welcoming Adult Inquirers

The preceding chapters of this volume have addressed a variety of theological, cultural, and practical issues surrounding the welcoming of adult inquirers into the life of a Christian congregation. What follows is a discussion of this welcoming as part of the congregation's ministry in daily life.

Welcoming inquirers or seekers is not incidental to the life of a Christian congregation. It is central because the proclamation of the gospel—from which the word "evangelism" receives both its power and its name—is central. Of course not everyone who walks through the door of a Christian congregation seeking answers to the basic and fundamental questions of faith and life is necessarily seeking Christ, yet in the very asking of primary questions Christ's church has something to offer. What we have to offer is death and new life in Christ.

Baptismal death and rebirth are at the heart and center of welcoming adult inquirers into a Christian congregation. This death and rebirth is a matter not only for the individual inquirer, but also for the congregation itself. Just as individuals must return daily to the waters of baptism for a daily dying and rising, so must a congregation. A Christian congregation models death and rebirth in its daily life—both in the lives of its individual members, and in its very identity as the body of Christ. Through that modeling our theology also becomes our ministry.

So how does this happen? How does a community of believers—a congregation—model death and new life? It happens in the regular preaching and teaching of a "life and death" baptismal theology. It happens in the clear proclamation of the word of God as both death and resurrection. It happens in the regular celebration of the sacraments—baptism and the Lord's supper—as central life and death events. It happens in the practice of worship, prayer, and the study of scripture. It happens wherever and whenever a Christian congregation lives out its daily death and rebirth in Christ through its ministry in daily life, which might include the following.

- Compassionate caregiving offered both to congregation members and members of the surrounding community;
- A social ministry centering on both justice and mercy;
- A good and faithful stewardship of congregational gifts and talents; and
- A focus on the mission and ministry of Christ as being central to everything that is part of congregational life.

A congregation models death and rebirth when

it dies and is reborn daily in the image of Jesus Christ, that is, when it lives not for itself, but for those in need—those for whom Christ lived and died.

There is also an individual ministry of modeling to those who are inquirers. If we take seriously our understanding of vocation as the living out of our baptismal calling both to love God and serve our neighbor, then there is a place for such a ministry of modeling in the life of a Christian congregation. This can take many practical forms, including the following examples.

- A small group called together for scripture study, and organized around a similar vocational "office" or role. (For example, teachers meeting in small group with other teachers—including inquirers—for study and discussion of the real-life decisions that teachers make on a daily basis.)
- A small group, centered on study of the lectionary (the regular scripture readings each Sunday) and called together on the basis of a shared concern. (For example, parents of children who suffer from illness, injury, or disease.)
- A working group—including inquirers—called together to live out a specific social ministry. (For example, a congregation or community sponsored food bank or shelter for the homeless.)
- A catechumenate or affirmer group—including leaders and pairs of sponsors and inquirers—meeting regularly for prayer, scripture study, and discussion of ministry in daily life.

Any of these examples would be appropriate settings for *either* unbaptized catechumens or baptized affirmers. Both catechumens and affirmers may be infants in the faith who would be served by a ministry of modeling. At the same time, this distinction must be maintained: catechumens are preparing to be joined to the death and rising of Christ in baptism, while baptized affirmers are returning daily to the death and rising that is already theirs in baptism.

Be What You See and Receive What You Are

We return to where we started. In preaching to the newly baptized on the Day of Pentecost, St. Augustine exhorted his hearers to "Be what you see, and receive what you are." What we see on the altar of the Lord's supper is what we are called to be—the compassion, love, and forgiveness of Jesus Christ—crucified and raised for the sake of the world. As Christ died and was raised for us, so we are called to such a ministry on behalf of others. Likewise, in the bread and wine of communion—the body and blood of Jesus Christ—we receive that which we already are. We are the body of Christ, called to new life out of a death that is also our birth. It is surely a mystery, but it is a life-giving mystery for which we give thanks.

---

1. St. Augustine, "Sermon 272" Migne P.L., 38:1246-1248. English translation from the Latin made at the request of the writer by Fr. Knute Anderson, St. John's Abbey, Collegeville, Minnesota, in March 1983.
2. Martin Luther, *A Contemporary Translation of Luther's Small Catechism,* trans. Timothy J. Wengert (Minneapolis: Augsburg Fortress, 1994), 29.
3. *Lutheran Book of Worship* (Minneapolis: Augsburg Publishing House, 1978), 70.
4. Martin Luther, "The Blessed Sacrament of the Holy and True Body of Christ, and the Brotherhoods," *Word and Sacrament I,* vol. 35, *Luther's Works,* American Edition ed. E. Theodore Bachmann (Philadelphia: Fortress Press, 1960), 58.
5. From parables such as "The Dishonest Manager" (Luke 16), "The Unforgiving Servant" (Matthew 18), and "The Talents" (Matthew 25), and from teachings such as "The Faithful and Unfaithful Slaves" (Matthew 24), a theology of stewardship arises.

Resources for Group Ministry

Preparation of Affirmers

*Confirmation, Reception into Membership, Restoration to Membership, Reaffirmation**

Welcome of Inquirers for Affirmation of Baptism	*Calling of the Baptized to Continuing Conversion*	*Affirmation of Baptism*	
INQUIRY *Inquirers*	**AFFIRMATION** *Affirmers*	**CANDIDACY** *Candidates*	**BAPTISMAL LIVING** *Newly Affirmed*
Inquiry is an open-ended period of time during which ***inquirers*** make an initial exploration into Christian faith and life. This period of inquiry is shaped by the inquirer as well as parish leaders and the congregation. Through a public order of welcome, inquirers are received as affirmers. This welcome may be celebrated at any time during the church year.	**Affirmation** is an open-ended period of time during which ***affirmers*** explore the Christian faith more deeply through the reading of scripture, prayer, worship, and ministry in daily life. This period of reflection and study may last from several months to a number of years. When affirmers are to be received into membership at Easter, they may participate in Calling of the Baptized to Continuing Conversion on Ash Wednesday, and an order of preparation on Maundy Thursday.	Especially when Affirmation of Baptism is to occur at Easter, Lent may be observed as a final six-week period of preparation for ***candidates*** who will affirm their baptism at Easter. Affirmation of Baptism may occur at the Easter Vigil or some other time during the Easter season. Since candidates for affirmation have already been baptized, they would ordinarily have been communicants since the time of Inquiry.	Easter may be observed as an intentional time of baptismal living. This period extends throughout the Fifty Days of Easter and beyond. *Affirmation of the Vocation of the Baptized in the World* A second order of baptismal affirmation may be celebrated during which the newly affirmed announce their vocation in the world. For those who affirmed their baptism at Easter, it is particularly appropriate to celebrate the Affirmation of the Vocation of the Baptized in the World on the Day of Pentecost.

Note: For a similar outline detailing the preparation for baptism, see *Welcome to Christ: A Lutheran Introduction to the Catechumenate*, p. 77.

*Though the order for Affirmation of Baptism in *Lutheran Book of Worship* does not include "reaffirmation" as a potential occasion for this service, it is possible that people who have previously affirmed their baptism would like to mark a life transition or maturity in faith through a repeatable order of affirmation. Such a possibility is mentioned in *The Use of the Means of Grace*, principle 30 and application 30A.

Outline and Topics for Affirmers Groups

Sessions may be 60–75 minutes each week. When the affirmers group will focus on readings from the Sunday lectionary, it may be helpful to meet directly following one of the congregation's weekly services, or later in the day on Sunday. An outline may be as follows:

- Prayer (perhaps the prayer of the day)
- (Topic)
- Bible study/reflection
- Prayer (several options include: prayer spoken by the leader, spontaneous petitions offered by group members, a summary prayer of the session, or the week's psalm read by the group)
- Announcements for the benefit of the group (be sure to indicate what readings will be used for the next gathering)

In addition to Bible study/reflection and prayer, the affirmers small group may include discussion of one or more topics in each session. Topics may range from various doctrinal issues to aspects of worship, the sacraments, and the daily life of a Christian. Topics may be ordered for their relationship to the lectionary for a given week or season. Topics presented to the group should not be in a lecture format, but rather should be offered in the form of a dialogue or conversation. Be aware that each group has different needs and interests. The topics presented might vary in number and in manner of presentation from group to group.

Possible topics include:

- Sin
- The Trinity (particularly as expressed in one or more creeds of the church)
- Grace
- Word
- Sacraments
- Prayer—devotional and corporate intercessory prayer
- Worship
- Ministry in daily life
- Mission
- Church history (an overview)
- Denominational history (particularly of one's own denomination)

Some helpful resources for the presentation of topics include the following printed materials that are listed in this book's concluding section on resources, p. 111:

Connections: Faith and Life
Gathered and Sent: An Introduction to Worship
Lutheran Basics
Luther's Small Catechism

Bible Study or Reflection Methods

A variety of Bible study or reflection methods are possible for affirmers group sessions. Word of Life, *part of the Life Together Series (see list of resources on page 111) is a weekly lectionary study for adults. Two popular models for scripture reflection are also printed below. Leaders should also feel free to create and adapt methods that work for them and for their groups.*

African Bible Study or *Collatio*

This method of scripture study is known in different circles by two names. The term *collatio* is derived from the Latin and refers to the process of "collecting" or gathering thoughts, reflection, and prayers through the hearing of a passage of scripture read multiple times. Another name for this method is African Bible Study, a reference to this practice among base Christian communities in South Africa. This method has been used with a great deal of satisfaction, especially when participants may have a limited reading ability. No matter what it is called, this method turns Bible study away from the intellectual pursuit of knowledge about the text and toward an attitude of listening to what God is saying through the text.

The outline of the process is adaptable at the discretion of the leader or the group, but it is important that the group share an understanding of the "ground rules." In a society that takes little time to listen, it may take some practice for people to learn to listen carefully to the scriptures. Sharing of insights is encouraged. Debate or arguing points of interpretation is discouraged. Respecting the offerings of each individual is important. The group should agree to maintain trust and confidentiality with one another.

- The leader begins with an opening word that reminds the participants that Christ is present where we are gathered in his name. The leader then invites each person to listen carefully to the word as it speaks to them.
- The leader speaks a prayer of invocation.
- The selected passage is read slowly, distinctly, with pauses that allow hearers to dwell on the text.
- The group keeps silence for a few minutes of reflection.
- Participants are invited to share briefly a word, a phrase, or an image from the text that catches their attention and speaks to their life at this time.
- The passage is read a second time, slowly and deliberately.
- Silence is kept for a few minutes.
- Participants are invited to share about how the text speaks to a place in their lives that is deeper or wider. "Deeper" means reflecting more deliberately about some aspect of self that is challenged, questioned, or affirmed by the text. "Wider" means reflecting on how the text speaks about the person's relationships with others including family, work, world.
- The passage is read a third time.
- Silence is kept for a few minutes.
- Participants are invited to speak a prayer that grows out of the text and their reflection on it. Sometimes the leader might encourage individuals to pray for themselves, and other times they might pray for others in the group.
- The leader closes the session with prayer or a hymn.

Visualizing the Text

In addition to hearing and reading a scripture passage, the affirmers can visualize the text. Seeing a text acted out or drawn on a flip chart can take the passage out of the two-dimensional words and into a three-dimensional picture. A text portrayed visually or by persons acting it out takes on new life. Dialogue or ideas take shape, literally! Relationships implied in the words of a text show up in visual relief. The group can even have fun by stretching a text into caricature in order to find the word that God addresses to them in the passage.

Almost any passage of scripture can be drawn or acted out. Parables of Jesus, stories from Acts, or accounts from the Old Testament provide a ready script. But the leader can help the group go beyond the initial impressions of the story by inviting them to stretch their perception of the passage. Notice the relationships and interplay of characters in the story. Then portray them using present-day language or with parallel images in today's society. Pay special attention to juxtaposition of characters. Draw the story in several frames in a cartoon format with "thought balloons" that express what is only implied in the words.

Other sections of scripture also lend themselves to visual expression. The psalms, the prophets, and many of the Pauline texts can be portrayed in drawing, acting, or sculpting as the story line of the passage is identified one phrase, image, or sentence at a time.

The point of visualizing a passage is to help affirmers see the word of God as it is: lively, active, and speaking to their lives here and now. They might find themselves in a character of the story, or in several characters. They might picture a truth about their own life that is illuminated by the acting out of the story. Because the catechumenate is about recognizing the call to faith and life in Christ, leaders can help the group find where the cross shows up in the story, either in fact or by asking what the story has to do with the death and resurrection of Jesus Christ.

Methods will vary according to the background, knowledge, and skills of the leader. Each affirmer group will develop its own sense of being together. Appropriate catechetical methods will help the group turn their attention to the word God is speaking to individuals and to the community of faith, to hear God's call to baptism and discipleship, and to respond affirmatively in faith.

Affirmers Leadership Team

Particularly in small congregations, one or more of these responsibilities could be assumed by a given individual, but there is a significant amount of work for a team to do in a good working affirmer process.

The following are the people who might be included in an affirmers team:

Small Group Coordinator

If there are several small groups of affirmers, a small group coordinator will be needed. If there are only a few groups, the small group guides or leaders will likely be members of the leadership team themselves.

Sponsor Coordinator

Sponsors need to be recruited and trained on a regular basis. They also need support throughout the affirmer process.

Pastors and Directors of Education

Pastors and directors of education need to be supportive of the affirmer process, even if they are not directly involved in a small group. Pastors and education directors also need to be able to guide the direction of the leadership team.

Hospitality Coordinator

This coordinator needs to create a welcoming environment for new members. Select rooms that provide comfortable furnishings and allow for easy conversation among group members. Chairs should be arranged in a circular fashion (not a classroom style with everyone facing in the same direction). Provide beverages and/or snacks if appropriate.

Liturgical Ministries Coordinator

Someone representing the worship planning process in your congregation needs to help coordinate the occasions when affirmers will be involved in various rites (Affirmation of Baptism, and those rites that may occur before and after affirmation—see the possibilities included in this book). Provide names of affirmers and sponsors to those who lead the congregation's prayers.

Communication Coordinator

People need to be personally invited and welcomed to participate in an affirmers group. In addition to telephone calls and face-to-face conversations with potential affirmers, be sure to send a letter detailing meeting times and spaces, and listing the names and phone numbers of any people who will be involved in leading the group. Bulletin, newsletter, and even Web site announcements are also needed for people in the congregation to be informed about this ministry and its schedule.

Volunteer Ministry Coordinator

Affirmers need to learn what possibilities exist for ministry within the congregation. Get to know their needs and interests. Provide information to affirmers about any congregational ministries and the work of other related organizations in the community at large. Follow up on their involvement within a few weeks of their initial interest in the congregation.

Excerpts from *The Use of the Means of Grace*

The following are excerpts from *The Use of the Means of Grace: A Statement on the Practice of Word and Sacrament,* which has been adopted for guidance and practice by the Fifth Biennial Churchwide Assembly of the Evangelical Lutheran Church in America, August 19, 1997. The following excerpts are from part two of the statement, the portion dealing specifically with the practice of baptism. While the entire statement is useful for congregations and individuals to study, the particular passages reprinted here are especially relevant to the scope of this volume.

BAPTISM IS ONCE FOR ALL

Principle

16 A person is baptized once. Because of the unfailing nature of God's promise, and because of God's once-for-all action in Christ, Baptism is not repeated.

Background 16a Baptism is a sign and testimony of God's grace, awakening and creating faith. The faith of the one being baptized "does not constitute Baptism but receives it. . . ." "Everything depends upon the Word and commandment of God. . . ."[25]

Application 16b "Re-baptism" is to be avoided[26] since it causes doubt, focusing attention on the always-failing adequacy of our action or our faith. Baptized persons who come to new depth of conviction in faith are invited to an Affirmation of Baptism in the life of the congregation.[27]

Application 16c There may be occasions when people are uncertain about whether or not they have been baptized. Pastors, after supportive conversation and pastoral discernment, may choose to proceed with the baptism. The practice of this church and its congregations needs to incorporate the person into the community and its ongoing catechesis and to proclaim the sure grace of God in Christ, avoiding any sense of Baptism being repeated.

---

25. The Large Catechism, Baptism, 53.
26. *Baptism, Eucharist and Ministry,* Baptism, 13.
27. The Large Catechism, Baptism, 47–63.

BAPTISM IS FOR ALL AGES

Principle

18 God, whose grace is for all, is the one who acts in Baptism. Therefore candidates for Baptism are of all ages. Some are adults and older children who have heard the Gospel of Jesus Christ, declare their faith, and desire Holy Baptism. Others are the young or infant children of active members of the congregation or those children for whom members of the congregation assume sponsorship.

Application 18a Since ancient times, the Christian Church has baptized both infants and adults.[33] Our times require great seriousness about evangelization and readiness to welcome unbaptized adults to the reception of the faith and to Baptism into Christ. Our children also need this sign and means of grace and its continued power in their lives. In either case, Baptism is God's gift of overwhelming grace. We baptize infants as if they were adults, addressing them with questions, words, and promises that their parents, sponsors, and congregation are to help them know and believe as they grow in years. We baptize adults as if they were infants, washing them and clothing them with God's love in Christ.

BAPTISM INCLUDES CATECHESIS

Principle

19 Baptism includes instruction and nurture in the faith for a life of discipleship.

Application 19a When infants and young children are baptized, the parents and sponsors receive instruction and the children are taught throughout their development. With adults and older children, the baptismal candidates themselves are given instruction and formation for faith and ministry in the world both prior to and following their baptism. The instruction and formation of sponsors, parents, and candidates prior to Baptism deals especially with faith in the triune God and with prayer. In the case of adults and older children this period of instruction and formation is called "the catechumenate." *Occasional Services* includes an order for the enrollment of candidates for Baptism.[34]

Application 19b The parish education of the congregation is part of its baptismal ministry. Indeed, all of the baptized require life-long learning, the daily re-appropriation of the wonderful gifts given in Baptism.

---

33. *Baptism, Eucharist and Ministry,* Baptism, 11–12.

34. *Occasional Services: A Companion to Lutheran Book of Worship* (Minneapolis: Augsburg Publishing House and Philadelphia: Board of Publication, Lutheran Church in America, 1982), 13–15.

SPONSORS ASSIST THOSE BEING BAPTIZED

Principle

20 Both adults and infants benefit from having baptismal sponsors. The primary role of the sponsors is to guide and accompany the candidates and, so far as possible, their families in the process of instruction and Baptism. They help the baptized join in the life and work of the community of believers for the sake of the world.

Application 20a Congregations are encouraged to select at least one sponsor from among the congregational members for each candidate for Baptism.[35] Additional sponsors who are involved in the faith and life of a Christian community may also be selected by parents of the candidate or by the candidate. Choosing and preparing sponsors requires thoughtful consideration and includes participation by pastors or other congregational leaders.

Background 20b The sponsors of children are often called "godparents." They may fulfill a variety of social roles in certain cultures. These roles may be regarded as an elaboration of the central baptismal role they have undertaken. Such sponsors take on a lifelong task to recall the gifts of Baptism in the life of their godchild.

Background 20c The sponsor provided by the congregation is, in the case of the baptism of an infant, especially concerned to accompany the family as it prepares for Baptism and, as a mentor, to assist the integration of the child into the community of faith as it grows in years. In the case of the baptism of an adult, this sponsor accompanies the candidate throughout the catechumenate, in prayer and in mutual learning, assisting the newly baptized adult to join in the ministry and mission of this community.

Application 20d The entire congregation prays for those preparing for Baptism, welcomes the newly baptized, and provides assistance to sponsors.

---

35. *Statement on Sacramental Practices*, Evangelical Lutheran Church in Canada, 1991.

BAPTISM IS REPEATEDLY AFFIRMED

Principle

30 The public rite for Affirmation of Baptism may be used at many times in the life of a baptized Christian. It is especially appropriate at Confirmation and at times of reception or restoration into membership.

Application 30a "When there are changes in a Christian's life, rites of affirmation of Baptism and intercessory prayer could mark the passage."[52] "Moving into a nursing home, beginning parenthood or grandparenthood, choosing or changing an occupation, moving out of the parental home, the diagnosis of a chronic illness, the end of one's first year of mourning, the ending of a relationship, and retirement are all examples of life's transitions that could be acknowledged by these rites."[53] Other examples include adoption and the naming of an already baptized child, release from prison, reunion of an immigrant family, and new life after abuse or addiction.

Application 30b Every Baptism celebrated in the assembly is an occasion for the remembrance and renewal of baptism on the part of all the baptized. The Easter Vigil especially provides for a renewal of baptism.[54]

---

52. *The Confirmation Ministry Task Force Report*, 9–10.
53. Ibid.
54. *Lutheran Book of Worship* Ministers Edition, 152.

Orders of Worship for Affirmers

WELCOME OF INQUIRERS FOR AFFIRMATION OF BAPTISM

This welcome of those inquiring into Christian faith and life may be used whenever there are baptized people who desire to begin a more public relationship with a Christian congregation. This rite is intended to be used during the principal Sunday service of the congregation.

Stand

PRESENTATION OF AFFIRMERS

At the door, before the entrance hymn, affirmers and their sponsors gather with the ministers to be welcomed by the congregation. The congregation faces the affirmers. The presentation of affirmers may also take place following the prayer of the day: the affirmers and their sponsors may be invited to stand at their places or to stand before the presiding minister.

The presiding minister addresses the congregation:

P Dear friends, we are gathered [at this door] today
to meet *these persons* who have been led by God's Spirit
to affirm *their* baptism.
Together, let us welcome *them* to this time of preparation and renewal.

When the alternate placement of this rite following the prayer of the day is used, the presiding minister's address should be adapted:

P Dear friends, today we meet *these persons*
who have been led by God's Spirit to affirm *their* baptism into Christ.
Together, let us welcome *them* to this time of preparation and renewal.

The sponsor for each of those preparing to affirm baptism says:

I present [name] to prepare for affirmation of Holy Baptism.

With these or similar words, the presiding minister asks each candidate:

P What do you ask of God's church?
R To be strengthened in faith and to affirm the covenant
God made with me in baptism.

P What do you seek from God's Word?
R Faith and fullness of life.

The presiding minister continues:

P Grace and mercy are given to all who call upon God's name.
We await your affirmation of baptism with joy.
Now I ask you, will you be faithful in learning the way of Christ?

Each affirmer responds:

R I will, and I ask God to help me.

The presiding minister addresses the sponsors and the congregation:
P Sponsors, you now present *these candidates* to us
in preparation for affirmation of baptism.
All of you who are assembled here are called
to support *these candidates* and *their sponsors*.
Will you help them hear the gospel of Christ
and be strengthened as members of the household of faith?
C We will, and we ask God to help us.

P Let us pray. Merciful God,
we thank you for *these* your *servants* [names]
whom you have made your own by water and the word in baptism.
You have called *them* today and *they* have answered you in our presence.
We praise you, O God, and we bless you.
C We praise you, O God, and we bless you.

The assisting minister continues:
A Now, [names], come and hear the word of God with us.

The service continues with the entrance hymn. The affirmers and their sponsors may join the entrance procession and take their places in the congregation together.

Sit

SIGNING WITH THE CROSS

Following the hymn of the day, the affirmers and their sponsors gather before the congregation.

The presiding minister addresses the affirmers with these or similar words:
P You have heard the holy and saving gospel of our Lord Jesus Christ.
Now receive the sign of that gospel, the sign given you in baptism,
on your body and in your heart,
that you may know the Lord and the power of his resurrection.

A sponsor traces a cross on the affirmer's forehead.
P Receive the ✠ cross on your forehead,
a sign of God's endless love and mercy for you.
Learn to know and to follow Christ.

One of the following or another response may be sung or spoken by the congregation.

**C Praise to you, O Christ,
the wisdom and power of God.**

Or

**C Glory and praise to you,
almighty and gracious God.**

The presiding minister may continue, with a sponsor or guide tracing a cross on each part of the affirmer's body as it is named.

P Receive the ☩ cross on your ears,
that you may hear the gospel of Christ, the word of life. *Response*

P Receive the ☩ cross on your eyes,
that you may see the light of Christ, illumination for your way. *Response*

P Receive the ☩ cross on your lips,
that you may sing the praise of Christ, the joy of the church. *Response*

P Receive the ☩ cross on your heart,
that God may dwell there by faith. *Response*

P Receive the ☩ cross on your shoulders,
that you may bear the gentle yoke of Christ. *Response*

P Receive the ☩ cross on your hands,
that God's mercy may be known in your work. *Response*

P Receive the ☩ cross on your feet,
that you may walk in the way of Christ. *Response*

PRESENTATION OF THE BIBLE

A representative of the congregation presents a Bible to each affirmer with these or similar words:

Receive this Bible.
Hear God's word with us.
Learn and tell its stories.
Discover its mysteries.
Honor its commandments.
Rejoice in its good news.
May God's life-giving word, sweeter than honey,
inspire you and make you wise.

Stand

BLESSING OF AFFIRMERS

The affirmers may kneel. The presiding minister may extend both hands over the affirmers or may lay a hand on each affirmer's head during the prayer.

The presiding minister continues with these or similar words:

P The Lord be with you.

C And also with you.

P Let us pray.
Merciful and most high God, creator and life-giver of all that is,
you have called all people from darkness into light,
from error into truth, from death into life.
We ask you: grant grace to [names] and bless *them*.
Raise *them* by your Spirit.
Revive *them* by your word.
Form *them* by your hand.
Renew in *them* the water of life and feed *them* with the bread and cup of blessing,
that with all your people *they* may bear witness to your grace
and praise you forever through Jesus Christ our Lord.

C Amen

The assisting minister concludes with these or similar words:

A God bring you in peace and joy to fullness of life in Christ
and to the affirmation of your baptism.

C Amen

The affirmers and their sponsors return to their places. One of the following or another response may be sung or spoken by the congregation.

C May the God of all grace
who has called you to glory
support you and make you strong.

Or

C Blessed be God
who chose you in Christ.
Live in love as Christ loved us.

The service continues with the prayers.

Notes on the Service

This rite is the adapted version of "Welcome of Inquirers to the Catechumenate" and is reprinted from *Welcome to Christ: Lutheran Rites for the Catechumenate.* The order printed here is intended only for those who are preparing for affirmation of baptism. If there are (also) adult candidates for baptism, the "Welcome of Inquirers to the Catechumenate" from *Welcome to Christ: Lutheran Rites for the Catechumenate* should be used.

This rite may be used to welcome those preparing to affirm their baptism. Every effort should be made not to regard the baptized as though they have not received the sacrament.

Music for the responses at the signing with the cross and after the blessing of affirmers is printed in *Welcome to Christ: Lutheran Rites for the Catechumenate.*

Suggested Hymns and Songs

The following hymns and songs may be used to support the Welcome of Inquirers.

LBW 104	In the cross of Christ I glory
LBW 250	Open now thy gates of beauty
LBW 365	Built on a rock
LBW 377	Lift high the cross
LBW 398	"Take up your cross," the Savior said
LBW 455	"Come, follow me," the Savior spake
WOV 718	Here in this place
WOV 719	God is here!
WOV 750	Oh, praise the gracious power
WOV 789	Now the feast and celebration
TFF 73	Jesus, keep me near the cross
TFF 146	I can hear my Savior calling
TFF 154	You have come down to the lakeshore

LBW: Lutheran Book of Worship; WOV: With One Voice; TFF: This Far by Faith

Calling of the Baptized to Continuing Conversion

This rite may be used as a part of the Ash Wednesday liturgy for those preparing to affirm their baptism at the Easter Vigil or on Easter Sunday.

After the confession, and just prior to the imposition of ashes in the Ash Wednesday liturgy, those preparing for affirmation of baptism come forward with their sponsors.

P Brothers and sisters in Christ,
on this Ash Wednesday
the whole church enters a time of remembering
our Lord's passion, death, and resurrection.
All who are in Christ
are called to journey with Christ
by keeping a holy Lent.
During this season,
as you prepare to affirm your baptism,
you are called, with all the baptized,
to continuing conversion,
to die daily to sin,
and to walk in newness of life.

Guide: [Names] are preparing for affirmation of baptism and will continue *their* preparation by joining with the entire congregation in keeping a holy Lent.

P As you prepare to affirm the promises you made to God in baptism,
you stand among us as *examples* of the calling we all have
to walk in the ways of Christ.
Therefore I ask of you, during this time of discipline and renewal:
Will you continue to hear the word of God
and receive it as a pattern for your *lives*?

R I will, with God's help.

P Will you continue to deepen your life of prayer
for all God's people in Christ Jesus,
and for all people according to their needs?

R I will, with God's help.

P Will you continue to join with the church in worship and service,
both in the community of faith and in the world,
by walking in love as Christ loved us and gave himself for us?

R I will, with God's help.

P Sponsors, and members of this congregation,
will you continue to support and pray for these candidates
as they continue their preparations for baptismal affirmation?

C We will.

P Let us pray.
Blessed are you, O Lord our God;
you have called your people
to do justice,
to love kindness,
and to walk humbly with you.
Bless [names] and all of your holy people
as we journey in faith this Lent.
Guide us to true repentance and renewal,
and to follow in the way of the cross;
through Jesus Christ our Lord.

C Amen

The imposition of ashes follows. Those preparing for affirmation of baptism are invited to kneel and receive the ashes. The minister applies the ashes to their foreheads with the words:

Remember that you are dust, and to dust you shall return.

The imposition of ashes continues with remaining persons in the congregation.

Preparation of Candidates for the Three Days

This rite may be used on Maundy Thursday with candidates for affirmation of baptism.

Candidates for affirmation of baptism are encouraged to take part in individual confession and absolution at some time prior to the celebration of this rite.

When this rite is used, the appropriate gospel is John 13:1-17, 31b-35. Before the washing of feet in the Maundy Thursday liturgy, those preparing for affirmation of baptism and their sponsors come forward and stand before the presiding minister.

The presiding minister addresses the candidates for affirmation.

P Brothers and sisters in Christ:
on the night before his passion,
in an act of humble service,
Jesus knelt down and washed the feet of his friends.
In so doing he modeled a way of life for all of us who believe.

Jesus said, "I have set you an example,
that you should do as I have done to you."
No servant is greater than the master;
therefore, those who are disciples
should accept such service from one another,
and continually model such service
in the ministry of their daily lives.

P [Names], you are preparing to affirm the covenant
God made with you in Holy Baptism.
We welcome you to join with the entire congregation
in dedicating *yourselves* anew to servant ministry,
to which all disciples of Jesus Christ have been called.

Tonight, we wash your feet as a sign of this servant ministry
and we ask that you in turn join us in this sign of discipleship.

The presiding minister washes the feet of the candidates for affirmation of baptism.

Appropriate hymns or songs may be sung by the congregation during the footwashing.

After their feet have been washed, candidates for affirmation of baptism receive basins, ewers, and towels to join in washing the feet of other members of the congregation.

The service continues with the prayers.

HOLY BAPTISM AND AFFIRMATION OF BAPTISM

This rite may be used when both baptism and affirmation of baptism are celebrated within the same service.

INTRODUCTION

While a baptismal hymn is sung, the candidates, sponsors, and parents gather at the font.

The minister addresses the baptismal group and the congregation.

P In Holy Baptism our gracious heavenly Father liberates us from sin and death by joining us to the death and resurrection of our Lord Jesus Christ. We are born children of a fallen humanity; in the waters of baptism we are reborn children of God and inheritors of eternal life. By water and the Holy Spirit we are made members of the church which is the body of Christ. As we live with him and with his people, we grow in faith, love, and obedience to the will of God.

PRESENTATION OF BAPTISMAL CANDIDATES

A sponsor for each baptismal candidate, in turn, presents the candidate with these or similar words:

I present [name] to receive the sacrament of Holy Baptism.

ADDRESS TO CANDIDATES AND SPONSORS

The minister addresses those candidates who are able to answer for themselves:

P [Name], do you desire to be baptized?
R I do.

When adults or older children and are baptized, the minister addresses the sponsors:

P In Christian love you have presented *these people* for Holy Baptism.
You should, therefore, faithfully care for *them* and help *them* in every way
as God gives you opportunity,
that *they* may bear witness to the faith we profess,
and that, living in the covenant of *their* baptism
and in communion with the church,
they may lead *godly lives* until the day of Jesus Christ.
Do you promise to fulfill these obligations?

The sponsors respond:
R I do.

If there are also infants or young children to be baptized, the minister says:

P In Christian love you have presented *these children* for Holy Baptism.
You should, therefore, faithfully bring *them* to the services of God's house,
and teach *them* the Lord's Prayer, the Creed, and the Ten Commandments.
As *they grow* in years, you should place in *their* hands the Holy Scriptures
and provide for *their* instruction in the Christian faith,
that, living in the covenant of *their* baptism
and in communion with the church,
they may lead godly lives until the day of Jesus Christ.
Do you promise to fulfill these obligations?

The parents and sponsors respond:
R I do.

PRESENTATION OF AFFIRMERS

Candidates for affirmation of baptism may be presented as follows:

CONFIRMATION

Confirmation marks the completion of the congregation's program of confirmation ministry, a period of instruction in the Christian faith as confessed in the teachings of the Lutheran church. Those who have completed this program were made members of the church in baptism. Confirmation includes a public profession of the faith into which the candidates were baptized, thus underscoring God's action in their baptism.

A representative of the congregation presents the candidates to the minister:

These persons have been instructed in the Christian faith and desire to make public affirmation of their baptism.

Their names are read.

P Dear friends, we rejoice that you now desire to make public profession of your faith and assume greater responsibility in the life of our Christian community and its mission in the world.

RECEPTION INTO MEMBERSHIP

Christians from other denominations become members of the Lutheran church through reception into the local congregation. In Holy Baptism they were made Christians; now they become members of the Lutheran church.

A representative of the congregation presents the candidates to the minister:

These persons have come to us from other churches, and desire to make public affirmation of their baptism.

Their names are read.

P Dear friends, we rejoice to receive you, members of the one holy catholic and apostolic church, into our fellowship in the gospel.

RESTORATION TO MEMBERSHIP

Baptized persons who desire again to participate actively in the life of the church are restored to membership through affirmation of their baptism.

A representative of the congregation presents the candidates to the minister:

These persons desire to make public affirmation of their baptism as a sign of their renewed participation in the life and work of the church of Christ.

Their names are read.

P Dear friends, we rejoice that you have returned to the household of God to claim again the eternal inheritance which is your birthright in Holy Baptism.

REAFFIRMATION OF BAPTISM

Persons who wish to reaffirm their baptism may also be presented at this time.

A representative of the congregation presents the candidates to the minister:

These persons desire to reaffirm their baptism as a sign of their renewal in the church's ministry and mission.

Their names are read.

P Dear friends, we rejoice that you have renewed your faith and that you have come to a deeper awareness of God's call in your life.

Stand

THE PRAYERS

When baptism and affirmation of baptism is celebrated within the liturgy of Holy Communion, the prayers may be said at this time, with special reference to those who will be baptized or who will affirm their baptism.

After each portion of the prayers:

A Lord, in your mercy,
C hear our prayer.

THANKSGIVING

The minister begins the thanksgiving:

P The Lord be with you.
C And also with you.

P Let us give thanks to the Lord our God.
C It is right to give our thanks and praise.

P Holy God, mighty Lord, gracious Father:
We give you thanks, for in the beginning your Spirit moved over the waters
and you created heaven and earth.
By the gift of water you nourish and sustain us and all living things.

By the waters of the flood you condemned the wicked
and saved those whom you had chosen, Noah and his family.
You led Israel by the pillar of cloud and fire through the sea,
out of slavery into the freedom of the promised land.
In the waters of the Jordan
your Son was baptized by John and anointed with the Spirit.
By the baptism of his own death and resurrection
your beloved Son has set us free from the bondage to sin and death,
and has opened the way to the joy and freedom of everlasting life.
He made water a sign of the kingdom and of cleansing and rebirth.
In obedience to his command, we make disciples of all nations,
baptizing them in the name of the Father, and of the Son, and of the Holy Spirit.

Pour out your Holy Spirit,
so that *those* who *are* here baptized may be given new life.

Wash away the sin of *all those* who *are* cleansed by this water
and bring *them* forth as *inheritors* of your glorious kingdom.
To you be given praise and honor and worship
through your Son, Jesus Christ our Lord,
in the unity of the Holy Spirit, now and forever.
C Amen

RENUNCIATION AND PROFESSION

The minister addresses the baptismal group, those affirming their baptism, and the congregation.

P I ask you to profess your faith in Christ Jesus, reject sin,
and confess the faith of the church, the faith in which we baptize.

P Do you renounce all the forces of evil, the devil, and all his empty promises?
C I do.

P Do you believe in God the Father?
C I believe in God, the Father almighty,
creator of heaven and earth.

P Do you believe in Jesus Christ, the Son of God?
C I believe in Jesus Christ, his only Son, our Lord.
He was conceived by the power of the Holy Spirit
and born of the virgin Mary.
He suffered under Pontius Pilate,
was crucified, died, and was buried.
He descended into hell.*
On the third day he rose again.
He ascended into heaven,
and is seated at the right hand of the Father.
He will come again to judge the living and the dead.

P Do you believe in God the Holy Spirit?
C I believe in the Holy Spirit,
the holy catholic Church,
the communion of saints,
the forgiveness of sins,
the resurrection of the body,
and the life everlasting. Amen

**Or*, He descended to the dead.

BAPTISM

The minister baptizes each candidate for baptism.

P [Name], I baptize you in the name of the Father,
The minister pours water on the candidate's head.

and of the Son,
The minister pours water on the candidate's head a second time.

and of the Holy Spirit. Amen
The minister pours water on the candidate's head a third time.

Or

P [Name] is baptized in the name of the Father,
The minister pours water on the candidate's head.

and of the Son,
The minister pours water on the candidate's head a second time.

and of the Holy Spirit. Amen
The minister pours water on the candidate's head a third time.

Sit

A psalm or hymn may be sung as the minister, the baptismal group, and those affirming their baptism go before the altar.

LAYING ON OF HANDS

P The Lord be with you.
C And also with you.

Those who have been baptized kneel. Sponsors or parents holding young children stand. The minister lays both hands on the head of each of the baptized and prays for the Holy Spirit:

P God, the Father of our Lord Jesus Christ,
we give you thanks for freeing your sons and daughters from the power of sin
and for raising them up to a new life through this holy sacrament.
Pour your Holy Spirit upon [name]:
the spirit of wisdom and understanding,
the spirit of counsel and might,
the spirit of knowledge and the fear of the Lord,
the spirit of joy in your presence.
C Amen

SIGNING WITH THE CROSS

The minister marks the sign of the cross on the forehead of each of the baptized. Oil prepared for this purpose may be used. As the sign of the cross is made, the minister says:

P [Name], child of God, you have been sealed by the Holy Spirit
and marked with the + cross of Christ forever.

The sponsor or the baptized responds: "Amen."

After all have received the sign of the cross, they stand.

CLOTHING WITH A BAPTISMAL GARMENT

A white garment may be given to each of the baptized. A representative of the congregation may say:

Put on this robe, for in baptism you have been clothed in the righteousness of Christ, who calls you to his great feast.

GIVING OF THE LIGHT

A lighted candle may be given to each of the baptized (to the sponsor of a young child) by a representative of the congregation who says:

Let your light so shine before others
that they may see your good works and glorify your Father in heaven.

PRAYER FOR PARENTS

When small children are baptized, the following prayer may be said:

P O God, the giver of all life,
look with kindness upon the *fathers and mothers* of *these children.*
Let *them* ever rejoice in the gift you have given *them.*
Make *them teachers* and *examples* of righteousness for *their children.*
Strengthen *them* in *their* own baptism
so *they* may share eternally with *their children*
the salvation you have given *them,*
through Jesus Christ our Lord.
C Amen

WELCOME

The ministers and the baptismal group turn toward the congregation; a representative of the congregation says:

Through baptism God has made *these* new *sisters and brothers members* of the priesthood we all share in Christ Jesus, that we may proclaim the praise of God and bear God's creative and redeeming Word to all the world.

C We welcome you into the Lord's family. We receive you as fellow members of the body of Christ, children of the same heavenly Father, and workers with us in the kingdom of God.

AFFIRMATION OF BAPTISM

The minister addresses those making affirmation:

P You have made public profession of your faith. Do you intend to continue in the covenant God made with you in Holy Baptism:
to live among God's faithful people,
to hear his Word and share in his supper,
to proclaim the good news of God in Christ through word and deed,
to serve all people, following the example of our Lord Jesus,
and to strive for justice and peace in all the earth?

Each person answers in turn:

R I do, and I ask God to help and guide me.

P Let us pray.

Those making affirmation kneel. A brief silence is kept so that prayer may be made for them.

P Gracious Lord, through water and the Spirit you have made these *men and women* your own. You forgave them all their sins and brought them to newness of life. Continue to strengthen them with the Holy Spirit, and daily increase in them your gifts of grace: the spirit of wisdom and understanding, the spirit of counsel and might, the spirit of knowledge and the fear of the Lord, the spirit of joy in your presence; through Jesus Christ, your Son, our Lord.
C Amen

FOR CONFIRMATION ONLY

The presiding minister lays both hands on the head of each person:

P Father in heaven, for Jesus' sake, stir up in [name] the gift of your Holy Spirit; confirm *his/her* faith, guide *his/her* life, empower *him/her* in *his/her* serving, give *him/her* patience in suffering, and bring *him/her* to everlasting life.

Each person answers: "Amen."

Stand

The ministers may exchange the peace with the baptized, with those who have affirmed their baptism, with their sponsors and parents, and with the congregation:

Peace be with you. R Peace be with you.

All return to their places.

The service continues with the offering.

Affirmation of the Vocation of the Baptized in the World

When set within the service of Holy Communion, this order is used following the post-communion canticle.

The service may be adapted to other liturgical settings or other places within the rite.

AFFIRMATION OF VOCATION

During the post-communion canticle, those affirming Christian vocation together with their sponsors gather with the ministers at the baptismal font or pool. They may carry their baptismal candles. These candles are then lit from the paschal candle by an assisting minister.

The presiding minister addresses the congregation with these or similar words:

P Dear Christian friends:
Baptized into the priesthood of Christ,
we are all called by the Holy Spirit
to offer ourselves to the Lord of all creation
in thanksgiving for all that God has done and continues to do for us.
It is our privilege to affirm those who are endeavoring
to carry out their vocation as Christians in the world.

A representative of the congregation says:

Through Holy Baptism our heavenly Father set us free from sin
and made us members of the priesthood we share in Christ Jesus.
Through word and sacrament we have been nurtured in faith,
that we may proclaim the praise of the Lord
and bear God's creative and redeeming word to all the world.

A sponsor presents each newly baptized person and gives a brief description of the area of service to be affirmed. Each person presented may briefly comment on the significance of this choice.

One of the following or another response may be sung or spoken by the congregation.

C May the God of all grace
who has called you to glory
support you and make you strong.

Or

C Blessed be God
who chose you in Christ.
Live in love as Christ loved us.

The presiding minister continues:
P [Names], both your work and your rest are now in God.
Will you endeavor to pattern your life on the Lord Jesus Christ,
in gratitude to God and in service to one another,
at morning and evening, at work and at play,
from this day until the day of your death?
R I will, and I ask God to help me.

The presiding minister continues with these or similar words:
P The Lord be with you.
C **And also with you.**

P Let us pray.
Almighty God,
by the power of the Spirit you have knit these your servants
into the one body of your Son, Jesus Christ.
Look with favor upon them in their commitment to serve in Christ's name.
Give them courage, patience, and vision;
and strengthen us all in our Christian vocation
of witness to the world and of service to others;
through Jesus Christ our Lord.
C **Amen**

BLESSING

The assisting minister continues with these or similar words.
A Go out into the world in peace;
be of good courage;
hold to what is good;
return no one evil for evil;
strengthen the fainthearted;
support the weak;
help the suffering;
honor all people;
love and serve our God,
rejoicing in the power of the Holy Spirit.

The presiding minister blesses the congregation.
P The almighty and merciful God, Father, + Son, and Holy Spirit, bless you now and forever.
C **Amen**

DISMISSAL

The assisting minister dismisses the congregation with these or similar words.
A Go in peace. Serve the Lord.
C **Thanks be to God.**

A hymn or postlude may follow.

Notes on the Service

In preparation for this rite, it is important that those affirming Christian vocation be given adequate time to reflect on their place in the body of Christ and the vocation that they wish to affirm. Such preparation would certainly include reflection on how God's gifts of baptism, absolution, and communion shape the life of the Christian in the world.

The description of the area of service need not be extensive. The pastor and/or catechist may wish to assist in preparing this description. This is also a suitable project for discussion in the small groups with the catechist following baptism or affirmation of baptism.

Music for the responses at the signing with the cross and after the blessing of affirmers is printed in *Welcome to Christ: Lutheran Rites for the Catechumenate.*

Suggested Hymns and Songs

LBW 160	Filled with the Spirit's power
LBW 161	O day full of grace
LBW 163	Come, Holy Ghost, God and Lord
LBW 459	O Holy Spirit, enter in
LBW 505	Forth in thy name, O Lord, I go
LBW 508	Come down, O Love divine
LBW 523	Holy Spirit, ever dwelling
WOV 682	Praise the Spirit in creation
WOV 684	Spirit, Spirit of gentleness
WOV 687	Gracious Spirit, heed our pleading
WOV 688	O Holy Spirit, root of life
WOV 752	I, the Lord of sea and sky
WOV 755	We all are one in mission
TFF 100	We praise thee, O God
TFF 101	Spirit of the living God
TFF 153	Guide my feet
TFF 244	Send me, Jesus

Blessings and Prayers for Affirmers Sessions

Prayers before Reading and Praying the Scriptures

Advent
Open your word to us, Lord God.
We wait for you and long to see your face,
for you are our rock, our safety, and our refuge.

Christmas
O Christ, enlighten my soul and heart with your never setting light;
guide me to reverence of you, O Lord,
for your commandments are the light of my eyes.

Epiphany
Almighty God,
your Son has driven away darkness
with the brightness of your grace.
Enlighten all those who hear the word of life
that they may be led by your truth and
walk in the brightness of the Morning Star,
Jesus Christ, in whose name we pray.
Amen

Lent
One thing I ask of the LORD;
one thing I seek;
that I may dwell in the house of the LORD
all the days of my life.
See *Psalm 27:4*

Easter
I love you, O Lord my strength,
O Lord my stronghold, my crag, my haven;
my God, my rock in whom I put my trust.
My shield, the horn of my salvation and my refuge:
You are worthy of praise.

After Pentecost

Open our ears, that we may hear your word.
Open our eyes, that we may see your way.
Open our lips, that we may declare your praise.
Open our hearts, that your life may dwell among us.

November

As a deer longs for running streams,
so longs my soul for you, O God.
My soul is thirsting for you, O God,
when shall I come to appear before your presence?
See *Psalm 42:1-2*

Prayers and Thanksgivings after Reading and Praying the Scriptures

Advent

My soul proclaims the greatness of the Lord,
my spirit rejoices in God my Savior,
who has looked with favor on his lowly servant.
From this day all generations will call me blessed:
the Almighty has done great things for me
and holy is his name.
God has mercy on those who fear him,
from generation to generation.
The Lord has shown strength with his arm
and scattered the proud in their conceit,
casting down the mighty from their thrones
and lifting up the lowly.
God has filled the hungry with good things
and sent the rich away empty.
He has come to the aid of his servant Israel,
to remember the promise of mercy,
the promise made to our forebears,
to Abraham and his children forever.

Christmas

Now, Lord, you let your servant go in peace:
your word has been fulfilled.
My own eyes have seen the salvation
which you have prepared in the sight of every people:
a light to reveal you to the nations
and the glory of your people Israel.

Epiphany

I put my trust in you, O God.
You grant your lovingkindness in the daytime;
in the night time your song is with me.
Send your light and your truth
that they may lead me.
Bring me to your holy hill
that I may go to your dwelling
and know the joys of your Son, Jesus Christ.
Amen

Lent

We thank you, holy Father, for your Name
which you have made to dwell in our hearts,
and for the knowledge, faith, and immortality
which you have made known to us through your living Word, Jesus Christ.
To you be glory forever and ever.
Amen

Easter

Your words are as sweet as honey.
Your words are the delight of my heart.
Alleluia.

After Pentecost

Your rain and snow come down from heaven, O God,
and they do not return until they have watered the earth,
making it sprout and grow.
Grant that your holy word take root in our lives
and accomplish in us your purposes,
through Jesus Christ our Lord.
Amen

November

As a swallow seeking a nest to hatch its young,
I am eager for your altar,
O Lord, my God.
In you, O God, my soul finds rest.
See *Psalm 84*

Prayers and Blessings to Conclude a Gathering of Affirmers

Advent

Devote yourselves to prayer,
and keep alert for the coming of the Lord.
The blessing of God, Father, Son, and Holy Spirit
keep you in peace.
Amen

Christmas

As God's chosen ones, holy and beloved,
clothe yourselves with compassion, kindness, humility, meekness,
and patience.
Let the word of Christ dwell in you richly.
See *Colossians 3:12, 16*

Epiphany
Lord God of hosts,
we look for the day when you will set a feast for all your people,
a feast of rich food and well-aged wine,
a feast where no one will hunger or thirst,
a feast of grace and mercy in your Son, Jesus Christ.
Amen

Lent
O Lord, look with love on all
who have been marked with the sign of the cross.
Lead them through the waters of baptism
and raise them up to new life with you,
that they may sing your praise
through your Son, Jesus Christ our Lord.
Amen

Easter
Lead a life worthy of your calling
with all humility and gentleness,
with patience,
bearing with one another in love,
making every effort to maintain the unity of the Spirit
in the bond of peace.
See *Ephesians 4:1-3*

After Pentecost
May God strengthen you in the power of the Holy Spirit,
so that you may know the love of Christ, now and forever.
Amen

November

Rejoice always, pray without ceasing,
give thanks in all circumstances.
May the God of peace keep you sound and blameless
at the coming of our Lord Jesus Christ.
The one who calls you is faithful,
and he will do this.
See 2 *Thessalonians 5:16-17, 23-24*

Additional Prayers and Thanksgivings for a Gathering of Affirmers

Your face, O LORD, do I seek.
Do not hide your face from me.
See *Psalm 27:8-9*

Blessed Lord,
you speak to us through the Holy Scriptures.
Grant that we may hear, read, respect,
learn, and make them our own.
May your word grasp us, help us,
and hold us in hope.
Amen

Almighty God,
draw our hearts to you,
guide our minds,
fill our imaginations,
and control our wills
so that we may be wholly yours
through Jesus Christ.
Amen

O Jesus,
be present with us
as you were present with your disciples.
Open to us the riches of your word
and enlighten us with your truth.
Amen

Good and gracious God,
send your word as good seed
into the fields of our hearts.
Let the gentle rain of your Spirit
bring to life the growth of faith within us.
Amen

The LORD bless you and keep you;
the LORD make his face to shine upon you,
and be gracious to you;
the LORD lift up his countenance upon you,
and give you peace.
See *Numbers 6:24-26*

May God be gracious to us and bless us
and make his face to shine upon us.
See *Psalm 67:1*

May the God of peace
make you complete in everything good
so that you may do his will,
working among you that which is pleasing in his sight,
through Jesus Christ.
See *Hebrews 13:20-21*

Be doers of the word, and not merely hearers.
See *James 1:22*

The grace of our Lord Jesus Christ be with all of you.
See *2 Thessalonians 3:18*

May the Lord of peace
give you peace at all times in all ways.
See *2 Thessalonians 3:16*

The grace of the Lord Jesus Christ,
the love of God,
and the communion of the Holy Spirit be with all of you.
See 2 *Corinthians 13:13*

[May] your love overflow more and more
with knowledge and full insight
to help you determine what is best,
so that in the day of Christ
you may be pure and blameless,
having produced the harvest of righteousness
that comes through Jesus Christ
for the glory and praise of God.
See *Philippians 1:9-11*

We must always give thanks to God for you,
brothers and sisters, as is right,
because your faith is growing abundantly,
and the love of every one of you is increasing.
See 2 *Thessalonians 1:3*

Beloved,
build yourselves up on your most holy faith;
pray in the Holy Spirit;
keep yourselves in the love of God;
look forward to the mercy of our Lord Jesus Christ.
See *Jude 20-21*

Peace be with you.
See *John 20:21*

Resources for Ministry with Affirmers

Participant Resources

Access Bible (NRSV). A Bible designed especially for use with people new to the faith or to Bible study.

Church Year Calendar. Minneapolis: Augsburg Fortress, annual dated. Lists weekly readings from the Revised Common Lectionary on one sheet of paper.

Connections: Faith and Life. Evangelical Lutheran Church in America, Division for Congregational Ministries, 1997. Series of four participant books and leader resources for small groups based on Luther's catechisms and focused on opportunities for ministry in daily life.

A Contemporary Translation of Luther's Small Catechism. Translation and Introduction by Timothy J. Wengert. Minneapolis: Augsburg Fortress, 1994.

Gathered and Sent: An Introduction to Worship. Participant book by Karen G. Bockelman. Leader Guide by Roger Prehn. Minneapolis: Augsburg Fortress, 1999.

Lutheran Basics. Minneapolis: Augsburg Fortress, 1998.

Word of Life. Life Together Series. Minneapolis: Augsburg Fortress, annual dated. A resource for lectionary Bible study with adults.

Children's Resources

Exploring the Sacraments with Young Children. Leader Sourcebook. Minneapolis: Augsburg Fortress, 1998.

My Place at God's Table. Child's Book and Family Book. Minneapolis: Augsburg Fortress, 1998.

A Splash of Welcome Water. Child's book. Minneapolis: Augsburg Fortress, 1998.

Welcome Water. Parent book. Minneapolis: Augsburg Fortress, 1998.

Worship Reference

Sundays and Seasons. Minneapolis: Augsburg Fortress, annual dated.

The Use of the Means of Grace. A Statement on the Practice of Word and Sacrament. Minneapolis: Augsburg Fortress, 1997.

Resources for Unbaptized Adults

Though intended primarily for use with unbaptized adults ("catechumens"), much of the contents of these resources will serve the needs of other inquirers as well.

Welcome to Christ: A Lutheran Catechetical Guide. Minneapolis: Augsburg Fortress, 1997.

Welcome to Christ: A Lutheran Introduction to the Catechumenate. Minneapolis: Augsburg Fortress, 1997.

Welcome to Christ: Lutheran Rites for the Catechumenate. Minneapolis: Augsburg Fortress, 1997.

Welcome to Christ: Preparing Adults for Baptism and Discipleship. Chicago: Evangelical Lutheran Church in America, 1998. Videotape; length: 18:43.

Periodical

Catechumenate: A Journal of Christian Initiation. Chicago: Liturgy Training Publications. Published bimonthly with articles on congregational preparation of older children and adults for the celebration of baptism and eucharist.

Additional Background

Browning, Robert L. and Roy A. Reed. *Models of Confirmation and Baptismal Affirmation: Liturgical and Educational Issues and Designs*. Birmingham, Alabama: Religious Education Press, 1995.

Griend, Alvin J. Vander and Edith Bajema. *The Praying Church Sourcebook,* second edition. Grand Rapids, Michigan: CRC Publishing Company, 1997.

The Catechumenal Process: Adult Initiation and Formation for Christian Life and Ministry. New York: Church Hymnal Corporation, 1990.

Starting Small Groups—and Keeping Them Going. Minneapolis: Augsburg Fortress, 1995. Though not specifically for new members, this book offers several helpful suggestions for the care and organization of small groups.

Trumbauer, Jean Morris. *Sharing the Ministry: A Practical Guide for Transforming Volunteers into Ministers*. Minneapolis: Augsburg Fortress, 1995.